HISTORY IN FLAMES

To what extent does our knowledge of the past rely upon written sources? And what happens when these sources are destroyed? Focusing on the manuscripts of the Middle Ages, *History in Flames* explores cases in which large volumes of written material were destroyed during a single day. This destruction didn't occur by accident of fire or flood but by human forces such as arson, shelling and bombing. This book examines the political and military events that preceded the moment of destruction, from the Franco-Prussian War and the Irish Civil War to the complexities of the Second World War; it analyses the material lost and how it came to be where it was. At the same time, it discusses the heroic efforts made by scholars and archivists to preserve these manuscripts, even partially. *History in Flames* reminds us that historical knowledge rests on material remains, and that these remains are vulnerable.

ROBERT BARTLETT, CBE, FBA, is Professor Emeritus at the University of St Andrews. His books include *The Making of Europe: Conquest, Colonization and Cultural Change 950–1350*, which won the Wolfson Literary Prize for History. He has written and presented three television series for the BBC, 'Inside the Medieval Mind' (2008), 'The Normans' (2010) and 'The Plantagenets' (2014).

HISTORY
IN
FLAMES

The Destruction and Survival
of Medieval Manuscripts

ROBERT BARTLETT

CAMBRIDGE
UNIVERSITY PRESS

Shaftesbury Road, Cambridge CB2 8EA, United Kingdom

One Liberty Plaza, 20th Floor, New York, NY 10006, USA

477 Williamstown Road, Port Melbourne, VIC 3207, Australia

314–321, 3rd Floor, Plot 3, Splendor Forum, Jasola District Centre,
New Delhi – 110025, India

103 Penang Road, #05–06/07, Visioncrest Commercial, Singapore 238467

Cambridge University Press is part of Cambridge University Press & Assessment,
a department of the University of Cambridge.

We share the University's mission to contribute to society through the pursuit of
education, learning and research at the highest international levels of excellence.

www.cambridge.org
Information on this title: www.cambridge.org/9781009457156

DOI: 10.1017/9781009457187

First published 2024

Printed in the United Kingdom by TJ Books Limited, Padstow Cornwall

A catalogue record for this publication is available from the British Library

*A Cataloging-in-Publication data record for this book is available from the
Library of Congress*

ISBN 978-1-009-45715-6 Hardback

Contents

Preface

Our knowledge of the period of European history conventionally called the Middle Ages rests, in a large part, on the writings that survive from that time, all of them hand-written (manuscript). This book explores cases in which large numbers of such manuscripts were destroyed in a day, not by accident of fire or flood but by human destructive force – arson, shelling and bombing. The first part of the book analyses the conditions for the production and survival of manuscripts: writing materials, script, speed of scribes, storage in libraries and archives, and discusses speculative survival rates. Then, after a look at some important manuscripts that survived by the narrowest of chances (we almost had a world without Grendel or Grendel's mother), the focus turns to the main subject: destruction of manuscripts and the loss of historical knowledge this entailed. Chapters 6 to 10 consist of detailed case studies, from France, Ireland, Italy and Germany, between 1870 and 1944, in which human violence resulted in massive destruction of medieval material (and later material, too, but I am writing as a medievalist). I have selected five spectacular cases which have common issues. Each chapter describes the political and military events that led up to the moment of destruction, the nature of the material that was lost and how it came to be where it was. Finally, more cheerfully, there is discussion of the heroic efforts made by scholars and archivists to save something from those catastrophes.

This book certainly does not attempt comprehensive coverage of this important topic. Some famous cases, such as the destruction of the library of Louvain University in 1914, are not discussed, since they have been covered very well in the English-language literature. The history of the destruction of books and records outside Europe is not treated; my linguistic limitations would not make it profitable. What the reader will find here are vignettes of some of the most spectacularly destructive examples of modern European violence that had as a consequence the loss, in most cases for ever, of parts of the history of the European past.

The annihilation of hundreds of years of records or thousands of priceless books in the space of a few hours is something that was made more likely by certain long-term historical developments, especially the dual role of the modern state as both curator and destroyer of the record of the past. As the state increased its powers and its ambitions, it undertook the centralization of archives and books, creating wonderful resources for research and sometimes saving documents and literary texts from neglect or destruction, but simultaneously making them vulnerable. They were vulnerable because they were concentrated in one place, and those places were often important urban centres and hence targets in the endless warfare between states that is a fundamental thread of European history. Moreover, as technology developed, states had at their disposal greater and greater destructive power. Simple arson can do a lot of damage to books and records, but explosives can do more. Modern European states have mostly been nationalist, and the interplay of nationalism and scholarship is two-edged. Nationalist impulses led to the creation of institutions dedicated to 'national' history, however that was defined, with an enormous increase in historical knowledge; nationalist impulses also led to the catastrophic shelling and bombing discussed in this book, which are all linked to national conflicts and national struggles of different kinds. Also important in this story is the rapid development in the nineteenth and twentieth centuries of technologies of reproduction, which allowed copies of manuscripts to be multiplied and hence made more widely known, and information to be preserved in facsimile or image in the event of destruction of the original. But there was a race between these technologies of conservation and the technologies of destruction, and the latter had a bigger war-chest.

I am very grateful to Brian McHenry for helpful conversation, to David Ganz and John Hudson for their careful and thoughtful reading of the text, and to the Inter-Library Loan staff of the University of St Andrews Library for their quick and untiring help. I am sure the end-product is much better because of this support and advice.

CHAPTER 1

Our Knowledge of the Past

O N 31 OCTOBER 1398 PHILIP OF COURGUILLEROY, master huntsman of the king of France, issued a business document acknowledging the receipt of 1,000 pounds from the vicomte of Rouen, a local royal official whose revenues were clearly being channelled into supplying dog food and suchlike for the king's hunting pack. How do we know this, something that happened well over 600 years ago? We know it because the document was eventually acquired by an insatiable manuscript collector of the time of Louis XIV and Louis XV, Pierre Clairambault (1651–1740). Clairambault was in charge of tracing and checking the genealogies of the French nobility, and he amassed a vast archive of material, some of it original records, some transcripts. This original document of 1398, issued by the king's master huntsman, and still bearing a trace of sealing wax, was incorporated into a volume of Clairambault's huge assemblage of material. Then came the French Revolution. The new revolutionary government had no interest in records of the ancestry of the French aristocracy, and, after Clairambault's material was nationalized in May 1792, it was decided to cull it. In June that year, 600 manuscript volumes from Clairambault's collection were burned in the Place Vendôme in the middle of Paris. Just as the revolutionary government abolished the

1

monarchy (on 21 September 1792) and started the calendar anew (22 September was the first day of Year One), so they turned the records of the French aristocracy into ash. An exception was made, however, for documents concerning title to property and for those 'which might be of interest to the arts and the sciences', which is presumably how the volume with the master huntsman's document squeezed by (it is now in the National Library in Paris, the *Bibliothèque nationale de France*). A receipt from a royal huntsman is not Magna Carta or the Declaration of the Rights of Man, but our picture of the human past must be built up from thousands of small pieces of information, as well as from the grand documents. And the public bonfire in the Place Vendôme in June 1792 destroyed many thousands of those small pieces of information. Rich material about the European past that was available on 1 January 1792 had ceased to exist by 31 December 1792.

This is how the past slips away from us. We can know a limited amount about the recent past from our own memories and by talking to people who are willing to share theirs, but these sources dry up within less than a hundred years. Beyond that, our knowledge of the past depends on the surviving physical remains. These remains can be solid objects, such as buildings, or traces, such as ancient pollen, both of which provide valuable information, but, if we want named people and details of events, we need a written record. And a written record is vulnerable. Unless it is inscribed on stone or metal, writing is flammable, liable to damage by flood and fungus, and attractive to rodents, not for the message it contains, which is unreadable to them (we assume) but because of its attractive medium – reeds, animal skin and other nutritious material. At the risk of stating the obvious, after 1400 no new fourteenth-century sources were created – but those that did exist faced the danger of destruction (as in 1792).

Our knowledge of the past, as far as it comes from written sources, is shaped by two variables – how much written material was produced in each period, and how much survives. For most of the human past, whether we believe that humanity began millions of years ago or merely tens of thousands of years ago, no written material was produced. This long period is what is called, or used to be called, 'prehistory', the time before 'history', a word that derives from the ancient Greek *historia*, meaning 'inquiry, account of inquiries, narrative'. Of course, it is possible to speak of 'human history' when referring to the time before written records, but that history will be different from the history that became possible with writing. We may be able to obtain ever more detailed knowledge of how Stonehenge was constructed, but we will never know the names of the builders. Once writing began, around 5,000 years ago, there was a wholly new gateway to the past. We do know the names of some of the rulers of the city-states of Mesopotamia in the third millennium BC. One of them was the first named person in human history.

Much of the earliest writing was addressed to the important question of noting down how many cows one had and was strictly practical, but writing was a medium that could be employed for much more: recording songs, myths and stories; giving laws a permanency that oral custom did not have; enshrining grants and contracts in a form that could be checked; handing on traditions ('tradition' means 'handing on'); and even for setting down the word of God. Hence, advanced literate societies came to have literature, law, documentation, historical writing and scripture. The more of these things a society had, the more evidence future generations would possess when they wished to have a picture of that earlier society – as long as that written record survived.

The survival rate for written evidence depends on several things. First, there is the material, the physical object itself. Over the course of human history many types of material have been used as writing surfaces: palm leaves, birchbark, wax tablets, and many other things, some more durable, some less so. Inscriptions on stone or metal can last for thousands of years, bringing us information about such subjects as the campaigns of the Pharaohs or the ancient rituals of the Umbrians (recorded on bronze tablets from Gubbio), but these are unusual and expensive forms of writing. Everyday writing forms, however, can also be long-lasting. Medieval European writing has its earliest roots in ancient Mesopotamia, where the first writing arose. This was on clay tablets, which survive well when baked, especially in dry climates. Hundreds of thousands of such tablets survive from the ancient Middle East (a fire in a modern library destroys books but is no such threat in an ancient Mesopotamian library since the tablets bake well). The information that this vast reservoir of material might give, however, remains mainly potential, since most of the tablets are still waiting to be transcribed and translated, and the number of people with the required linguistic skills is small. Here is a field where the past will continue to be produced for decades to come.

Subsequently, papyrus, made from the reeds of the river Nile, became a common writing material. It was lighter than clay but also more vulnerable, since it could be torn or burned. It was written on, in ink, as distinct from having marks impressed into clay, and papyrus sheets were often made into scrolls, which could be of considerable length (the word 'volume', like the word 'roll', originally signified something that was revolved, like a scroll). The papyrus scroll was the form in which the literary works of ancient Greece and Rome were first circulated and in which texts were studied in the ancient schools. In hot, dry climates papyrus can last for centuries, and archaeological excavation in Egypt and elsewhere has turned up thousands of papyrus scrolls and fragments of scrolls. At Oxyrhynchus, south of Cairo, excavations began in 1896 and continued as more and more discoveries were made – something like half a million items have been found at this site, dating from the third century BC to the eighth century AD, a period of more than a thousand years. By 1900 there was even a new word, 'papyrology', to describe the study of this newly discovered material. Papyrus discoveries have thrown light on the culture of the ancient world, the everyday life of cities, the Bible, both Hebrew and Christian (the word 'Bible' derives from the Greek for 'papyrus') and the early days of Islam.

For medieval Europe, which is the focus of this book, the next step was of fundamental importance. This was the replacement of papyrus by parchment and the replacement of the scroll by the book (the codex). Parchment is specially treated animal skin (sheep, calf or goat), so the shift from papyrus represented a move from vegetable to animal material – there is even a tenth-century reference to parchment as 'animal papyrus'. Whereas clay tablets and papyrus required specific climatic conditions, or at least benefited from them, animal skin can be found anywhere, and animals had developed it specifically to withstand the elements. The different kinds of skin had different qualities: for example, English Exchequer records were ordered to be kept on sheepskin, since it was believed that an erasure – forging the text – was more obviously visible on sheepskin, a point supported by scientific analysis of 645 legal deeds from the sixteenth to twentieth centuries, virtually all of which were on sheepskin. However, the preparatory treatment was basically the same. The skin was made ready for writing by removing the hair and flesh through a process of soaking in lime and scraping, then stretched and dried on a frame, before being smoothed by further scraping and polishing with pumice. The resulting parchment is tough.

Even after parchment had become the usual writing material, however, there were other choices. A great deal of writing was done on wax tablets, that is, flat pieces of wood with a wax coating on which a sharp tool could scratch letters. This practice originated in very ancient times, and wax tablets were extremely useful for note-taking and short texts that did not need to be permanent. Many literary works were drafted on wax before being copied onto parchment. Naturally, only a few of these wax records survive. And, for long, papyrus continued to have special uses. It was employed by the popes for their more solemn documents, even though they had to go to the Muslim world to get it – a bull of Pope John VIII from 876 in favour of the monastery of Tournus in Burgundy is on papyrus that still bears the Arabic inscription naming the Egyptian official in charge of papyrus manufacture (since he ceased to be in office in 838, this papyrus must have been almost forty years old when the pope used it for his document). However, although there are papal bulls on papyrus as late as 1057, in general, parchment became dominant long before this and continued to be so throughout the Middle Ages.

The other major development of the late Roman period, the codex, is so much taken for granted that its oddity has been forgotten: rectangles of parchment or (later) paper, with writing on both sides, bound together to a spine, so that the pages may be turned, the whole usually contained in stiff covers. When it is shut, no light reaches the pages; it can be opened at any point; one sees at a glance how long it is. These are specific properties, different from both scrolls and our modern screens (it is significant that one 'scrolls' through a screen). One great advantage of the codex was that, when closed, the writing on the individual sheets was protected. This is especially important for the hand-painted illustrations that are one of the glories of medieval culture. Because they were not subject to light and because they were kept flat (either upright or horizontal) and because they were supported by boards and binding, the state of preservation of some illuminated manuscripts is astonishing. Some look just as they did when they were finished many centuries ago.

The earliest surviving fragment of a parchment codex was found at Oxyrhynchus, and is dated to around AD 100.

By the fourth century, the parchment codex had become by far the dominant form in which texts were transmitted. This triumph of the codex coincided with the triumph of Christianity, and naturally people wonder if there is a connection, since it is clear that the codex was the preferred form for Christian texts in the Roman period. One theory is that, since the Jewish Torah (Law) was in the form of a roll, the Christian choice of the codex might have been intended to mark the difference between the new Christian religion and its progenitor, Judaism. Another explanation is that the early Christians, from lower-middle-class backgrounds, were used to the codex format, since this was employed for workaday notebooks, ephemeral jottings, short letters, and suchlike, while scrolls were identified with the elite and their sophisticated literary reading. Whatever the explanation, the combination of parchment as material and codex as form was established by the beginning of the Middle Ages. While it is perfectly possible to make a codex of papyrus and to make a roll of parchment (indeed, most of the English royal records of the Norman and Plantagenet kings are in the form of parchment rolls), the typical medieval book is a parchment codex. Indeed, while the Middle Ages can be defined in many ways, with differing starting and ending points, one label for the period could be the Age of the Parchment Codex.

The material on which the writing was placed – clay tablets, papyrus scrolls or parchment books, all with different qualities – clearly influenced its chances of survival. Another major factor was the number of copies that were made. Obviously, the more copies of a text there were, the greater the chances of its being transmitted down the generations.

Every piece of writing on parchment was manuscript, that is, 'written by hand', so subject to the physical limitations of how much a human hand could copy.

There is some evidence of how fast scribes worked. One elderly scribe – he mentions that he is 71 – recorded the progress he made in copying out the 227 folios of the compendium of French history known as the *Great Chronicles of France* (*Grandes Chroniques de France*). He started his work in May 1469 and finished on 6 December 1469, copying an average of a folio or two a day, though clearly not working every day. His manuscript has 50 lines to a page, so if he copied out 2 folios (4 pages, a folio being the front and back of a single page), he would have produced 200 lines, and 200 lines a day is considered 'relatively rapid'. The *Great Chronicles* were, in medieval terms, a popular work, with 120 manuscripts surviving, representing more than 60 years of copying at the rate of our elderly scribe. Others worked faster. Professional university scribes at this time might produce between eight and sixteen folios in a week. Christine de Pisan, the extraordinarily productive writer active in France in the late fourteenth and early fifteenth centuries, copied out many of her own works, and in one of them she noted proudly, 'Here begins one quire written completely in a day.' A quire of eight folios (which was standard) was indeed an impressive day's work, when the average daily rate of production was two or three folios.

In addition to the speed of the scribe, the number of scribes would also be significant. There is a vivid description of 'an abundance of scribes' that the monastery of St Martin in Tournai enjoyed in the time of Abbot Odo (1095–1105): 'if you

Figure 1. Illustration of Christine de Pisan copying out her work *Livre de la mutation de fortune* (1403); she noted in this manuscript that she had copied out one whole quire in a day. Royal Library of Belgium MS 9508, fol. 2.

entered the cloister, on most occasions you would see twelve young monks sitting in their chairs and writing in silence at tables which had been carefully and skilfully constructed.' Under the supervision of the prior, they produced copies of the works of the Church Fathers – Ambrose, Jerome, Augustine, Gregory the Great, Isidore of Seville and Bede – as well as those of their contemporary, Anselm. Their work was so good, wrote a later abbot, 'that you could scarcely find a library its equal in any of the neighbouring churches, and they all requested copies from our church in order to correct their books.'

Monks did not usually expect to be paid for their scribal work, but, after the European university came into existence, around 1200, a whole new market was born, and with it a new profession, the full-time urban scribe. Students needed copies of the standard texts, and these could be provided efficiently by the so-called *pecia* system (*pecia* just means 'piece'). A stationer would produce an accurate master-copy of a text, which would not be bound but kept in loose quires usually of four folios. These individual quires would then be rented out to copyists for a week, who would copy them, return them and collect the next quire (these manuscripts were carefully numbered). In this way many scribes could be copying a text simultaneously. The universities attempted to regulate prices and procedures. Paris also supported a book trade beyond the university. Books were displayed for sale in the street outside the west front of Notre-Dame, while on the Left Bank there was a 'Street of Scribes'; rich and powerful patrons commissioned romances, saints' Lives and histories in French. Roughly contemporary with these developments was the emergence of the professional notary in several parts of Europe. Notaries were scribes with official authorization (commonly from the pope or Holy Roman Emperor) to draw up legally binding documents, which they authenticated not with a seal but with an elaborate 'sign manual', a complex design in ink that, it was hoped, could not be forged. In the trading cities of northern Italy, notaries drew up contracts; when the papacy investigated cases for canonization, they recorded the interrogations and witness statements. Thousands of volumes of notarial acts survive from the medieval period.

Late medieval Europe saw two developments that made it more familiar with written material than earlier periods. One was the use of paper, which was manufactured from cloth, not from animal skin. It was cheaper than parchment, and faster to write on (on average, more than 30 per cent faster). The other development also involved speeding up the process of writing. This was the more widespread use of cursive handwriting, in which the letter forms are written without the pen leaving the page ('joined-up writing') and is hence quicker to write than non-cursive. Cursive had been a familiar kind of handwriting in the Roman empire and was by no means an invention of the later Middle Ages, but it did become more common in that period than in earlier medieval centuries. Both the adoption of paper and the increased use of cursive contributed to growth in the amount of written material in circulation.

Paper spread very gradually across medieval Europe. It had been invented by the Chinese in the first or second century BC, arrived in the Muslim world in the eighth century AD and eventually came to Christian Europe. In Byzantium, the earliest surviving imperial document on paper dates from 1052, and the earliest dated paper manu-script from 1105, while a monastic library catalogue from a century later lists 267 parchment and 63 paper manuscripts, that is, almost 20 per cent of the total. Paper came to western Europe first in the form of imports from the Islamic world, then through the takeover of the paper industry in conquered parts of Muslim Spain, finally through the construction of paper mills in Italy in the thirteenth century. From the later part of that century, Fabriano near Ancona became a centre of paper production and export, and this is probably the city where watermarks were invented, those distinguishing marks impressed into the paper during manufacture that can help identify the place and date of production. The first evidence of paper mills in France and Germany is from the fourteenth century. There is no evidence of paper in England before 1300. The first paper mill in the country was established by John Tate, a merchant of Mincing Lane, London, who, by the 1490s, was producing paper, marked with his watermark (an eight-pointed star set in a double circle) at his mill in Hertford. The technique had taken 1,600 years to reach England from China.

The price difference between parchment and paper was obvious to contemporaries, especially those buying books. In his correspondence negotiating the purchase of a Bible, a fifteenth-century scholar put it very clearly: 'if it is paper, I will give eight florins, if it is parchment, twice that.' The price difference did not mean paper was shoddy. Medieval paper was not, in fact, especially poor quality or liable to decay. It has been pointed out that 'fifteenth-century paper survives today in much better condition than the great majority of book papers manufactured in the twentieth century'.

All these developments – paper, cursive, the multiplication of written texts – culminated in the invention of printing with moveable type in the 1450s, something that transformed the copying process. By the sixteenth century a press could produce as many as 1,500 double-sided printed sheets a day. It was now possible to create 120 copies of a text without the 60 years of laborious penmanship. Printing is, almost by definition, a marker of the end of the Middle Ages. The English politician and essayist Francis Bacon (1561–1626) regarded three inventions, unknown to the ancient world and of recent origin, as defining his own time: printing, gunpowder and the navigator's compass. 'These three things', he wrote, 'have indeed changed the face and condition of the world: the first has transformed literature and letters, the second warfare, the third navigation. No empire, no religion, none of the stars [meaning astrological influence], has had a greater impact on human affairs than these technologies.' Incidentally, he also believed that these inventions showed the superiority of Europe, which is a shaky claim, given that gunpowder and the compass, to say nothing of some form of printing, were known in China earlier than in Europe. But the claim that printing changed the face of the world is quite defensible. Between 1450 and 1600, 345,000 separate titles were printed in Europe, representing 100,000,000 individual copies (of which 1,500,000 survive). Mechanical reproduction transformed the basic framework of literacy.

It is possible to print on parchment, but it is far easier to print on paper. In his work *In Praise of Scribes*, the German abbot Johannes Trithemius (1462–1516) emphasized the greater durability of parchment: 'Who does not know how great is the difference between a manuscript and a printed work? For a manuscript written on parchment will last a thousand years; a printed work, however, since it is on paper, how long will it last? If a paper volume lasts two hundred years, that is something remarkable.' This did not stop him from organizing a printed edition of *In Praise of Scribes*, on paper. But even if Trithemius' point about the durability of parchment is true, when a medieval work that existed only in one manuscript was printed, even in a small print run, the chances of its survival were greatly multiplied.

And there are examples of medieval works that survive only in print. For instance, in the early thirteenth century, a monk of the Cistercian Order, Helinand of Froidmont (Froidmont abbey is a short distance south-east of Beauvais in northern France), wrote a very substantial chronicle in forty-nine books (subdivisions), covering the period from the Creation to 1204. Today there are only two surviving medieval manuscripts containing any part of this work, and neither has more than the first section. One is a thirteenth-century volume which has books 1–18, dealing with biblical and ancient history. It originally came from the Cistercian monastery of Beaupré in rural Picardy, then passed through the hands of Parisian book collectors before being purchased by the eccentric and bibliophile queen of Sweden Christina, and, after her abdication and retirement to Rome, coming into the book collection of the papacy. The book is still in the

Vatican library, with shelf-mark Reginensis latinus 535 ('Reginensis latinus' means 'the queen's Latin book'). The other manuscript was produced in either England or France early in the fifteenth century and originally formed the first part of a three-volume set containing the whole of Helinand's history. It was owned by Henry V of England and donated by his son, Henry VI, to King's Hall, Cambridge, which became part of Trinity College in the sixteenth century, and it then somehow passed into the library of Sir Robert Cotton, and hence into the British Library (Cotton and his collection is discussed in Chapter 4 below). Neither of these manuscripts contains any later part of Helinand's chronicle. There was, however, such a manuscript still available in Froidmont in the seventeenth century, and it was this that the Cistercian scholar Bertrand Tissier printed in 1669. It contains books 45–9, the last section of the chronicle, covering the years 634–1204, and, since the manuscript from Froidmont has since disappeared, it is its only record. Copies of this printed text survive to the present day in at least ten libraries, in France, Germany, Switzerland, Denmark and Britain, as well as on microfilm in Texas and Minnesota. In this case, printing, the innovative technology created in the fifteenth century, has saved some of the thirteenth-century past. As Marshall McLuhan, the famous historian of printing, pointed out, 'the sixteenth and seventeenth centuries saw more of the Middle Ages than had ever been available to anybody in the Middle Ages'.

For the preservation of the medieval past, the next great leap forward in technology occurred in the nineteenth century. After the invention of photography in the 1820s and

1830s, it was possible to make exact facsimiles of medieval manuscripts of all types, and thus provide a new kind of safeguard against destruction. Just as there are examples of medieval works surviving only in the form of early modern printed editions, so there are several examples of medieval works that now exist only in the form of nineteenth- or twentieth-century photographic reproductions (as we shall see later, in Chapters 9 and 10). And the latest step in the process of safeguarding medieval manuscripts is digitization. Hopefully, the technology for retrieving digital images will not become antiquated and get lost, like the ability to read Mesopotamian clay tablets. Otherwise, the late twentieth and early twenty-first centuries will be a new Dark Age.

CHAPTER 2

Libraries and Archives

APART FROM THE MATERIAL ON WHICH WRITING WAS inscribed and the number of copies made, another thing that affected the survival of books and documents is where they were stored. When considering this subject, it is common to make a distinction between libraries and archives, that is, between collections of books, perhaps kept on shelves but, in the medieval period, just as likely to be in cupboards, and collections of documents, including many single sheets, often stored by itinerant kings in chests or other portable containers. This categorization into libraries and archives can be helpful, as long as it is recognized that it is not always clear-cut. To take a modern example, the monastic cartularies of medieval England, in which thousands of documents are transcribed and which might presumably be classified as archive material, are now much more likely to be found in the British Library than in the National Archives. But, in general, it is true in the modern world that there are, on the one hand, depositories that house great collections of books, and others that house mainly administrative and governmental materials. In Paris one finds the National Library and the National Archives (the *Bibliothèque nationale de France* and the *Archives Nationales*), in Vatican City the Vatican Library and the Vatican Archives (the *Bibliotheca Apostolica Vaticana* and the *Archivum Apostolicum Vaticanum*, formerly *Archivum Secretum Vaticanum*), though in neither case is there a great distance to walk between them. The medieval precursors of such depositories are, on the one hand, monastic, court and university libraries, and, on the other, the government records stored in castles or churches, or taken with the royal court on its travels, or, sometimes, taken home by officials.

Christianity, like Judaism and Islam, is a religion of the book, and any community of Christians would have to be provided with at least a few books, but the greatest body of books in medieval Europe was to be found in the monastic libraries. There were thousands of monasteries, and many of them had collections of hundreds of books. Naturally, many of these books were liturgical, service books for the endless round of religious ceremonies that structured the lives of monks, but there were also library books, and not only biblical and theological texts but also history, grammar and poetry, as well as law and science. In theory, the great churches were undying institutions and might be presumed to be safe homes for books, but disruptions such as Viking raids, the Protestant Reformation and the secularizations of the late eighteenth and nineteenth centuries dispersed or destroyed many monastic book collections, and only a portion survives to the present.

Rulers also had the wealth to accumulate books but, in general, lacked the institutional continuity and simple physical stability that a great monastery provided. Many medieval kings were itinerant, perhaps moving two or three times a week, and this would inhibit their bibliophilic urges. Moreover, a ruler's successor might well not share their predecessor's interest in books, and collections which had no dedicated patron tended to be dispersed or be damaged. However, if there was a royal capital which was the king's usual residence, circumstances for book collecting were more favourable. Charles V of France (1364–80), a famous bibliophile, had a collection of over 1,200 manuscripts, in Latin, French and other languages, most of them housed in a specially remodelled wing of the royal palace of the Louvre in Paris, which contained three rooms, each with a large solid door and windows protected against birds by a trellis of brass wire. The librarian was a trusted servant of the king called Gilles Malet, who held the position from at least 1369 until his death (long after the king's) in 1411. One of his tasks in 1373 was to draw up an inventory of the books in the Louvre, and this is organized by subject: Bibles, psalters, Bible commentary, liturgy (including coronation rituals), private prayer books (books of hours), works of the Church Fathers, theology, devotional literature, Roman Law, French customary law (only five volumes), canon law, natural history, ethics and politics (including multiple copies of Giles of Rome's treatise on rulership, *The Government of Kings* (*De Regimine Principum*), which had been composed for Philip IV of France, great-grand-uncle of Charles V), mathematics, astronomy and astrology (a very large portion of the library), divination, medicine, geography, hagiography, history, Ovid and other Roman poets, romances and songs. On balance, it is a devotional and practical collection rather than one for relaxation or entertainment. The astrological books were particularly important, because kings, above all people, needed to know what was coming next in this uncertain world: Charles' father had been captured in battle by the English and spent much of his reign in captivity in England, and Charles' son, Charles VI, went mad, presided over a civil war and disinherited his own son. In the disturbed conditions of his reign, the library of Charles V was not preserved in Paris. Most of it was sold in 1425 to John, duke of Bedford, the representative of English power in France, and was then dispersed on the duke's death in 1435, though a hundred or so of the manuscripts can be traced and identified today. This short life of royal and princely libraries was typical, even if they did not all suffer the dramatic fate of the book collection of Mattias Corvinus, king of Hungary (1458–90). The largest royal library of its time, with 2,000–2,500 manuscripts, it fell into the hands of the Ottoman sultan after the conquest of Budapest by the Turks in 1526, and 90 per cent of the books have disappeared.

In the later centuries of the Middle Ages, universities and colleges might also have book collections, although most of these never came close to the size and scope of the great monastic libraries. When, in 1439, the University of Oxford received a gift of 120 books from Humphrey, duke of Gloucester, brother of John, duke of Bedford, just mentioned, the university thanked him effusively, 'since no king or prince in time past has given such a great and ample benefaction . . . except for King Alfred' (their reputed founder). Part of Oxford's Bodleian Library is still called Duke Humfrey's Library after him. In Paris, on the other hand, the Sorbonne, a college founded in 1257 for students of theology, built up a substantial collection of books in its early years, mainly from gifts and bequests of its alumni. By 1290 it had 1,017 books. Around this time the collection was divided into two sections:

the 'common library' or 'great library', containing copies of standard texts chained in place, which obviously had to be consulted in the library, and the 'small library', housing books that circulated (a chained library collection was a new idea at this time). Along with teaching materials and standard texts of reference, the Sorbonne also had some very rare works, including the Latin translation of Plato's *Phaedo*, the work in which Socrates discusses the immortality of the soul immediately before he takes the lethal cup of hemlock to which he had been sentenced. The Italian humanist Petrarch acquired a manuscript of the work, copied from that in the Sorbonne: the library thus was part of a chain transmitting the thought of ancient Athens to the Italian Renaissance.

Medieval catalogues, like those of the great monastic collections or the library of Charles V or the Sorbonne, provide one of the most important sources of information about libraries of the time. The long-term project to edit medieval British library catalogues had, by 2020, recorded 40,000 copies of individual works. Even so, for various reasons, catalogues may not constitute a full guide to the books held in the institution that drew them up. For example, books on loan might not be recorded, or specialist books might be missed out if kept separately from the main collection, as happened frequently in the big churches, where service books would be in the church, not in the library. Moreover, what of the hundreds of medieval monasteries that left no lists of books? Twenty medieval catalogues survive from the diocese of Augsburg, but there are surviving medieval manuscripts that demonstrably come from ninety different libraries in that diocese.

In addition to books, collections of documents of a practical and legal nature were accumulated by monasteries, rulers, corporate bodies such as towns and universities, and by individuals, especially landowners and merchants, and the volume of such material increased exponentially over the Middle Ages as writing became more and more an essential tool of government and administration. Some of these records were disposed of when no longer of use, others were dispersed on the death of the holder, but others became part of permanent archives, whose interest might eventually cease to be practical and become historical. There were administrators who thought archives were a precondition for good government. In 1323, the English royal treasurer, writing, as he said, for 'rulers and governors of lands who desire to rule well and guide the people subject to them justly', recognized that 'the fragility of the human condition' did not allow them to fulfil these admirable intentions 'unless the deeds and acts pertaining to their government are recorded in writings and other trustworthy memorials'. Taken seriously, this view implied that a safe home had to be found for this vulnerable written material, and consequently permanent record depositories came into existence. Kings often housed their records in churches or, from the twelfth century, entrusted them to the hands of the crusading Orders (Templars and Hospitallers), who were not only undying corporations but also had great experience in international finance.

There are some lucky archives which have survived from the Middle Ages without major cataclysms. One of the richest is the Archive of the Crown of Aragon in Barcelona, which houses the records of Aragon, Catalonia, Valencia and associated domains. Until the early fourteenth century royal documents had been preserved in monasteries in Aragon or in the houses of the crusading Orders in Barcelona, but in July 1318 James II of Aragon commanded the construction of 'a house with a vault in the place where the chapel of his palace was in Barcelona, in which the records, privileges and other writings of his chancery, and other matters of his court, might be placed and preserved'. A full-time archivist was appointed in 1346. The archive has a continuous history from that time. Other national archives are modern creations but have inherited or acquired documents from the medieval period. For instance, the French National Archives, founded in 1790, possess a papyrus document from 625, while the Public Record Office, which was founded in London in 1838, took custody of the Domesday Book of 1086 twenty years later. These 'Public' or 'National' archives, established by the modern state, took the place of royal archives and became symbols of institutional continuity and eventually great powerhouses of historical research.

Apart from such material as surveys and lists, the documentary archives of the Middle Ages can be classed as either records of incoming or of outgoing documents. Individuals and institutions had a natural interest in preserving documents they received if these granted them lands or rights, and hence the great churches of medieval Europe treasured such documents, so we see the creation of what can be called 'beneficiary archives', collections of documents of various kinds and dates and from various sources but all for one beneficiary. In rare cases, their archives still exist. The south Italian monastery of La Cava was founded in the early eleventh century and over the centuries has survived many threats to its existence and changes in its status. It still preserves around 15,000 parchment documents, some of which date to a period even before the monastery's foundation and came into its possession by various routes (the earliest is from 792). Publication of these documents, starting with the earliest, began in 1873 and still continues – a classic instance of a scholarly enterprise that transcends the lifetime of any individual scholar.

Grants of lands or rights of this type were recorded in charters, single-sheet parchments with authenticating features such as seals or the names of witnesses. But single sheets are subject to all sorts of dangers, and the great churches might copy out the texts of the individual parchment sheets they received into manuscript volumes, known as cartularies (more than a thousand cartularies survive from England alone). These obviously could not have the authenticating seals, but they preserved the texts, as well as consolidating them in one accessible place. Hemming, compiler of a cartulary for the bishopric of Worcester around 1100, explained his purpose: 'I have compiled this little book of the possessions of our monastery so that it should be clear to those who come after us which landed properties should rightfully belong to this monastery.' Sometimes the texts of the charters were integrated into a historical account of the church, producing a form called the cartulary-chronicle. And copying out charters into a cartulary also provided an ideal opportunity to 'improve' the text of the charter by adding details of properties that the monastic scribe knew truly belonged to his monastery but somehow had no written authority – this is not to mention out-and-out fabrication. Scholars who deal with medieval charters must have as their first task the critical discrimination between genuine charters, the 'improved' versions and the forgeries. But forgery is itself historical evidence: why, when and on what basis were such forged documents produced?

Apart from these beneficiary archives, some institutions and individuals felt the need to keep a record of outgoing documents. As in so many other areas of administration and bureaucracy, the popes seem to have been the first on the scene. A good example emerges from the pages of the Anglo-Saxon scholar Bede (d. 735). When he was writing his *Ecclesiastical History of the English People*, which he completed in 731, he had some practical help from the priest Nothelm (later to be archbishop of Canterbury), who not only brought him information about the early days of the Church in England that had been provided by contacts at Canterbury but also consulted the papal archives in Rome: 'coming to Rome, Nothelm searched carefully through the archives [*scrinium*] of the holy Roman church, with the permission of Pope Gregory who now presides over that church, and found there several letters of the blessed Pope Gregory along with those of other popes'. The 'Pope Gregory who now presides' is Gregory II, while the 'blessed Pope Gregory' mentioned here is Pope Gregory I ('the Great'), whose pontificate dates to 590–604, so these letters had been preserved for well over a century and were available to researchers like Nothelm generations later. They were of especial importance to Bede, since it was Gregory I who sent the first Christian mission to the Anglo-Saxons in 596–7. Gregory's letters in the Roman archives had been recorded on papyrus, one roll or book (it is unclear which) for each of the fourteen years of his pontificate, a record of outgoing correspondence. These were still in the archive in the ninth century, though none of them survives today. Fortunately, copies of Gregory's letters had been made from an early date, so the texts of 854 letters are now available to be studied and cast light on this energetic and important pope of the early Middle Ages.

The next surviving register of outgoing papal correspondence is from the pontificate of Pope John VIII (872–82): it is not the original but an eleventh-century copy, covering only the last six years of the pontificate and containing 314 letters, plus 61 fragments from other sources. The earliest surviving original papal register, rather than a later transcript, is that of Pope Gregory VII (1073–85), with 390 items, a priceless source for the ecclesiastical and political history of the late eleventh century. It is still in the Vatican Archives. From the time of Pope Innocent III (1198–1216), the series of papal registers is unbroken. Before that time, apart from the isolated peaks of the letters of Gregory the Great, John VIII and Gregory VII in the sixth, ninth and eleventh centuries respectively, papal documentation has to be painstakingly reconstructed from the archives of hundreds of recipients (the foundations for this work were laid by Philipp Jaffé in his *Regesta Pontificum Romanorum*, first published in 1851, which summarized more than 11,000 papal documents from the period before 1198).

The distinction between beneficiary archives and outgoing documentation comes out very clearly from the way the scholarly project 'English Episcopal Acta', which was initiated in the 1970s, is organized. The plan is to publish all the documents issued by English bishops before the first registers for that particular diocese begin. Bishops' registers, recording their business, began to be kept in England in the early thirteenth century, and when they survive give us a very good idea of the ordinary daily activities of a bishop. But, before that, a bishop's activities, as far as they are recorded in documents, have to be reconstructed by combing through the archives of all those institutions that might have received some grant or letter from the bishop. Hence there is a period when episcopal documents have to be reconstructed from beneficiary archives and then, from the thirteenth century, a new archival era when we have records of outgoing business.

Two short case studies from the reign of the emperor Frederick II can illustrate this difference between archives kept by the recipients of documents and copies preserved by those issuing them. Frederick, who died in 1250, ruled both the kingdom of Sicily (which covered southern Italy in addition to the island of Sicily), inherited from his mother, and the (Holy Roman) Empire, which at this time included the entire area of modern Germany, Austria, Switzerland, the Netherlands and the Czech Republic, plus parts of Poland, Belgium and eastern France, and northern Italy from the Alps to Rome. These vast territories were governed partly by delegation of authority to local nobles, bishops and cities, partly by the emperor's constant journeying through his domains, but also through the written word.

In June 1226 Frederick II, as emperor, issued a grand charter (21 inches by 18 inches, or roughly 54 centimetres by 45 centimetres) for the church of St Mary, Aachen (which is now Aachen cathedral). He recalled the foundation of the church by his famous predecessor, Charlemagne, and the favour shown to it by his own father and grandfather. He then confirmed its extensive possessions, listing them by name. It is almost certain that this list was provided by the clergy of St Mary's – it is unlikely that Frederick's courtiers and advisers knew where Gemmenich, Gulpen or Mook were (small places in modern Belgium and the Netherlands). The document concludes with the names of the witnesses (twelve bishops, two abbots and three great nobles), the emperor's mark, and the date and place of issue. The document was issued in Borgo San Donnino (now called Fidenza), a north Italian town between Parma and Piacenza, so it must have been carefully transported across the Alps and then down the Rhine towards Aachen.

Obviously, this document was of great importance to St Mary's, and the clergy of the church not only treasured it but also obtained confirmation of its terms from later German rulers. Since St Mary's was the traditional place of coronation, this ceremony provided a good opportunity to approach the newly crowned monarch with a request for such a confirmation (as seems to have happened in 1292, 1298, 1309, 1314 and 1349). The church kept these confirmation charters alongside Frederick II's original. However, a small error crept into the text, with the confirmations giving the date of issue as July 1226 not June 1226 – a tiny slip but a good indication of the way that copies are not always entirely faithful. The first time Frederick's charter appeared in print was in 1829, in a volume of local history by the Catholic priest, teacher and librarian, Christian Quix. His

Figure 2. Document of Frederick II for Aachen, 1226. State Archives of North Rhine-Westphalia – Rhineland Department – AA 0103 Aachen, St Mary's documents, No. 47.

text was based on seventeenth- and eighteenth-century transcripts of the confirmation of 1309 (and hence dated July 1226).

Before that, for more than 600 years, the transmission of the text had depended entirely on copying by hand.

In 1688 and 1743, when local notaries had made the transcripts on which Quix based his text, they found the confirmation charter still in the archives of St Mary's, and one presumes the other charters were there too. They formed part of a beneficiary archive, containing the documents issued *for* St Mary's, not *by* St Mary's. Today, these charters are all in the public archives of the German state of Nordrhein-Westfalen. It is remarkable that, through all the enormous political changes and destructive wars that modern Germany has experienced, these pieces of medieval parchment were handed down intact. In 1794, revolutionary French armies occupied Aachen and other areas west of the Rhine, and within a decade France annexed them, turning them into French départements, and closing down and appropriating hundreds of religious establishments. The archives of St Mary's, Aachen, went into the departmental archive of the Roer, based in Aachen. After the defeat of Napoleon, this area was given as the prize of war to Prussia, forming part of the 'Rhine Province' (this is why Karl Marx, from Trier, which was also part of the province, was born a Prussian subject), and the archives went into the care of the Prussian state. These archives had different names and locations over time, but Frederick's charter was in Düsseldorf for almost 200 years, until the reorganization of the archives of the Land of Nordrhein-Westfalen (itself created in 1946) in 2004, when it went into the branch of the Archive of the State of Nordrhein-Westfalen based in Münster (*Landesarchiv Nordrhein-Westfalen, Abteiling Rheinland, Westfalen*), where it now is, about 125 miles (200 kilometres) from St Mary's, Aachen, the church that received it 800 years ago. The fact that this document of 1226 survives to this day in the original is itself not to be taken for granted. We have the texts of 542 documents that Frederick II issued in the years 1220–6, but only 151 survive in the original, that is, in the physical form as they were written, sealed and despatched by Frederick's clerks, not as later copies. Our knowledge of the other 391 depends on the activities of copyists over the centuries. So roughly 72 per cent of the known documents that this powerful and relatively long-lived ruler issued in those years come down to us only as copies.

The charter of 1226 is a document preserved in an incoming archive, Aachen. The only record of outgoing documents from Frederick's reign that survived to modern times is a fragment from the register of his chancery for the year 1239–40. This did not contain solemn and permanent grants, like that to St Mary's, Aachen, but recorded terse instructions to royal officials in the kingdom of Sicily – to provide support for a royal slave who is learning to read and write Arabic, to make arrangements for the custody of the prisoners taken at Frederick's great victory over the north Italian cities at Cortenuova in November 1237, to buy better clothes for his son, Henry, who had been imprisoned after rebelling. Unlike the document issued for St Mary's, Aachen, which conveyed rights and property, and hence gave the recipient an interest in preserving it, the material in the register is of only transient interest, does not record permanent grants and therefore had no natural party interested in preserving it. By the seventeenth century, this fragment was all that survived of Frederick's registers, and the antiquarians of that time had no more to go on when studying such material.

There are occasional citations from this register to be found in the work of Neapolitan antiquaries but no full edition until 1786, when Gaetano Carcani, head of the royal printing press in the kingdom of Sicily (also known as the kingdom of Naples), published the register as an appendix to his edition of the laws of Frederick II. Despite occasional criticisms of his editorial work, Carcani had taken a major step in securing the survival of this important historical source. He was a scholarly man, expert in both Latin and ancient Greek, and a member of the Academy of Herculaneum, a learned society founded in 1755 under royal patronage and inspired by the study of the recently uncovered city, victim, like Pompeii, of the eruption of Vesuvius. Carcani's service to the king and his scholarly activities were to be disrupted by the revolutionary times in which he lived. In December 1798 French republican troops conquered the mainland part of the kingdom of Sicily. The king, Ferdinand, and his family managed to escape on a British warship (commanded by Horatio Nelson) and sought refuge in the island part of the kingdom. In January 1799 a republic, known as the 'Parthenopean Republic', was declared in mainland Naples, and this lasted until June, when a series of French defeats and the return of Ferdinand led to a bloody restoration. Champions of the republic were executed, imprisoned or exiled. The commander of the republican fleet was hanged at the yardarm of Nelson's flagship. Carcani, despite his earlier royal employment, had been a firm supporter of the republic, issuing printed documents on its behalf and being addressed as 'Citizen Carcani' by the French commander, but his punishment was less severe, only exile for life. He made his way to France, living by publishing Italian grammars, by teaching and, from 1807–11, by employment as head of the municipal library at Nantes. In 1810, he composed a hymn in Greek to celebrate the marriage of Napoleon and Maria Louisa of Austria. Eventually he was restored to his position as head of the printing house in Naples. Throughout all this, the manuscript of Frederick's register remained in the archive of the kingdom at Naples, being transferred to its new location in the church of St Severinus and St Sossius in 1845, along with the rest of the Great Archive of the Kingdom (*Grande Archivio del Regno*). The manuscript survived the downfall of Frederick II's dynasty and the chaos of the revolutionary and Napoleonic wars, and looked as if it had a safe home in a public archive.

The history of this fragment of the register shows something of the way national identities can shape the study of medieval history. Although Frederick II was born in Italy, died in Italy and spent 72 per cent of his reign in Italy, he was nevertheless a ruler of special significance to modern German historians. His father was the emperor Henry VI, his grandfather the emperor Frederick I, nicknamed 'Barbarossa' (the word which was chosen as the code name for the German invasion of the Soviet Union in 1941). These rulers were members of a family known as the Staufer in German and conventionally as the Hohenstaufen in English. They were among the most powerful rulers of their time and left an imprint in historical memory and in legend. The contemporary chronicler Matthew Paris called Frederick II 'the wonder of the world'. Soon after Frederick's death in 1250, new 'Fredericks' were turning up, claiming to be the lost emperor and leading serious risings against the established powers. Frederick's magic continued in the twentieth century, famously in Ernst Kantorowicz's 1927 volume on the emperor, which was translated into English a few years later, preserving the elevated tone of the original – 'his life and strife to the last hour did not lack glory', Frederick was 'the seducer, the deceiver, the radiant, the merry, the ever-young'.

It was thus not surprising that German medievalists devoted themselves to Frederick, lured by his charisma and perhaps also by the warm climate of Italy. A natural home for them was offered by the Prussian Historical Institute in Rome, founded in 1888, soon after the French and the Austrians had founded their historical institutes in that city. In 1907 the young scholar Eduard Sthamer (1883–1938) was given a position there and began work on the medieval documentation of the buildings of Frederick II and his successors. This was a topic partly inspired by the interest in the subject that Kaiser Wilhelm II had developed after being given a tour of the castles of southern Italy by the Director of the Prussian Historical Institute. Sthamer soon settled in Naples in order to work in the archives there and began publishing studies on the castles of the kingdom of Sicily, although he was forced to leave Italy after that country entered the First World War on the opposing side. In the 1920s, now able once more to visit Italian archives, he turned his attention to the fragment of Frederick II's register preserved in the Naples State Archive, which he undertook to edit for the Monumenta Germaniae Historica, the venerable institution dedicated to publishing the medieval sources for the history of Germany and the Holy Roman Empire. Sthamer died in 1938 without his edition

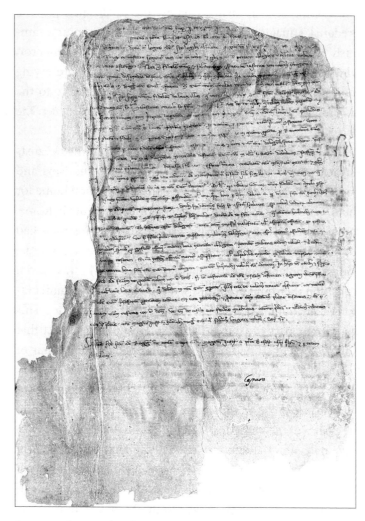

Figure 3. Photographs of the destroyed fragment of the Register of Frederick II, taken in the 1930s. State Archive of Naples, photograph from the estate of Friedrich Sthamer, c. 1940, Munich, MGH-Archive K 123/V.

having been published, but his typescript transcription is preserved in the German Historical Institute (successor to the Prussian Historical Institute) in Rome. Two years after Sthamer's death, Wilhelm Heupel, also working for the Monumenta Germaniae Historica, had the register photographed, and these photos still exist, in the Monumenta's archive in Munich. Neither Heupel nor – as we shall see in Chapter 8 – Frederick II's register survived the destruction of the Second World War. So, this fragment of the outgoing documentation of one of the most powerful rulers of the Middle Ages is known now only through an eighteenth-century printing, a typescript in Rome and old photos in Munich.

CHAPTER 3

What Has Been Lost?

WHEN WE INVESTIGATE A PERIOD FOR WHICH THE sources are sparse (which are sometimes labelled 'Dark Ages'), it is not always possible to say to what extent the sparseness is to be explained because that period produced very little written material or because that which was produced was destroyed for some reason. On occasion, however, we can make reasonably informed estimates of the rate of loss of material that once existed. An example is provided by the drama of ancient Greece. Six or seven of Aeschylus' tragedies have survived to the present day (one is of disputed authorship). The number of other tragedies that he wrote but that have disappeared is not quite certain, but one careful survey lists fifty-nine lost tragedies, established on the basis of ancient lists, citations in other works or surviving fragments. This means about 90 per cent of his tragedies have disappeared.

Another case where we can get a general impression of the extent of lost material is the Byzantine empire. This was one of the most powerful and sophisticated states of the medieval world, especially prior to the fall of Constantinople to errant crusaders in 1204, and had a high level of literacy and a developed bureaucracy. In Byzantium it was customary to seal letters and documents with lead seals, which were imprinted with images and inscriptions. Because they were made of lead, as distinct from the wax used in the West, Byzantine seals survive in the thousands, even though the documents they were attached to have perished. The important centre for Byzantine studies at Dumbarton Oaks in Washington, DC, has 17,000 seals, and that is simply one depository. In comparison, very few Byzantine documents survive. It has been pointed out that 'Anglo-Saxon England has left a richer documentary heritage than Byzantium', despite the fact that Byzantium was bigger, richer and lasted longer. Hence, we can conclude that the Byzantine empire produced thousands and thousands of documents that have disappeared. Part of the explanation of the disappearance of these documents is the destruction of the Byzantine state after the Turkish conquest of 1453. The old state would have had an interest in safeguarding and archiving these documents, but the new state did not. Conquest, especially if involving changes in language and religion, as this one did, is often a cause of the loss of written record, through neglect if not through destruction. Similarly, in the generations after the Norman Conquest of England in 1066, once people were no longer able to read Old English, the impetus for the copying of Old English texts – both documents and literary works – diminished, and many disappeared.

We have a welcome guide to what was being read by educated Byzantines in the ninth century, in the form of Photius' *Bibliotheca*. In this work, Photius, who was Patriarch of Constantinople (858–67 and again 877–86), summarized and gave his opinion on hundreds of Greek works of ancient and medieval times, with an emphasis on history, saints' lives, philosophy and theology. The number of works it covers can be calculated in different ways, but it certainly approaches 300. In 2017, Tim O'Neill undertook a thorough analysis of this list, reckoning that it contained a total of 294 books, and worked out how many still existed today, concluding that 107 books are extant and 187 lost, that is, 36 per cent extant, 64 per cent lost. So, there is roughly a two-in-three chance that these works, being read in ninth-century Byzantium, have disappeared in the last thousand years or so.

It is natural to assume that written material created long ago has a worse survival rate than that produced more recently, but that is not invariably the case. A book catalogue from Würzburg cathedral from around 800 lists thirty-six volumes, of which twenty still survive, representing a loss rate of 44 per cent. The catalogue made in the fifteenth century for St Augustine's Canterbury, a major Benedictine monastery, records just under 1,800 volumes. Of these, fewer than 200 survive. So, 1,600 are no longer extant, a loss rate of around 90 per cent, far worse than the rate for the German book collection catalogued 700 years earlier, a fact doubtless to be explained by the thoroughness of the dissolution of English monasteries under Henry VIII. The libraries of England's medieval monasteries were scattered at the Reformation, and the bulk of their books lost. This was lamented even by Protestant champions like John Bale, who considered it would have been preferable to establish a library in each county where 'the chief monuments and most notable works' could have been preserved, and thought that 'to destroy all without consideration is and will be unto England for ever a most horrible infamy'. It is clear from their library catalogues that medieval English monasteries housed thousands of books but, as the great manuscript scholar Neil Ker put it succinctly and categorically, 'extant books are no guide whatever to the actual contents of the medieval libraries'. Only shards and scraps have survived. The project to edit British medieval library catalogues reckons that 85 per cent of the books listed in the catalogues do not now physically survive.

Such catastrophes, however, were not always the fate of libraries when monasteries or other ecclesiastical establishments were suppressed, and it is instructive to look at the procedure in later, eighteenth- and nineteenth-century, secularizations of monasteries and churches. While England under Henry VIII saw an aristocratic feeding frenzy, with the lands and treasures of the monasteries being grabbed, squabbled over and plundered, later secularizations were often more orderly, and regulated by state authorities who saw themselves implementing rational and enlightened policies. This was clearly the approach of Joseph II of Austria, when he ordered the closure of more than 700 monasteries in the 1780s. After 1789, when the French revolutionaries nationalized the libraries of the Church, the Crown and the aristocracy, the plan was that the books should be sent to central storage sites in each district to be assessed and catalogued, and that those suitable should then be placed in newly created public libraries (rather as Bale had suggested). Since neither the money nor the personnel were available for the swift and complete execution of such a giant project, books sometimes mouldered in their storage sites or disappeared – parchment was in demand to make the cartridges containing the powder and shot for firearms – but, nevertheless, many medieval manuscripts made their way into public libraries in this way (the case of Chartres is discussed in detail in Chapter 10).

After French power had extended as far as the Rhine in the years 1797–1801, it was agreed that those German princes who lost territory would be compensated by the grant of monasteries, cities or smaller aristocratic lordships within Germany east of the Rhine. As a result, there was a vast programme of secularization, inevitably involving the dispersal of the monastic and ecclesiastical libraries. In Bavaria, a 'Library Commission' was set up in February 1803 to oversee this process, headed by Johann Christoph von Aretin, a member of a Bavarian noble family, a legal and historical scholar and also a librarian at the Court Library of the Elector of Bavaria in Munich. He and his colleagues had the task of touring Bavaria to select books from the confiscated libraries. Manuscripts, early printed books and costly items were reserved for the Court Library; 'useful books' were to be sent to the University of Landshut (this university later moved to Munich) or to the gymnasia (advanced secondary schools); 'superstitious books' were to be destroyed – this category included many of the books from the libraries of the friars. A Munich paper manufacturer offered to buy the condemned books for a fixed price per hundredweight (50 kg) and acquired 94 tons to be used in the production of new books, etc. The transfer of material was enormous. It has been calculated that, because of the secularization, the Bavarian Court Library acquired around 600,000 volumes, including 'one of the most important manuscript collections in the world'. Even today, the class marks of the Latin manuscripts in the

Bavarian State Library (successor to the Court Library) follow the alphabetical sequence of the ecclesiastical institutions from which they came, grouping all the manuscripts from one church or monastery in a continuous series. The contrast with the chaos of the English Reformation is clear.

Neither the production nor the destruction of manuscripts proceeded at a uniform or predictable rate. The transmission of manuscript books encountered certain moments when, if texts were not copied, they ceased to exist. A notable example is the Carolingian period (meaning basically, for this subject, the ninth century), which was of fundamental importance in the transmission of ancient Roman literature. It was a boom period for manuscript production in comparison with preceding centuries. As the palaeographer David Ganz wrote, 'Some 500 manuscripts survive from Merovingian Gaul copied before c. 750: some 7,000 manuscripts survive copied in the Carolingian empire between c. 750 and 900.' The choices of what to copy made at this time determined what would be transmitted. In general, one can say that if ancient Latin literature was not copied in the Carolingian period, it is not likely to survive.

Because English medieval records are rich, and because they have been the subject of imaginative interpretation, it is possible to produce a pair of graphs illustrating rates of both production and survival of documents of the English royal government in the thirteenth century. The calculation of survival rates of English eyre rolls, that is, the parchment rolls that recorded the activities of the royal judges who went on periodic visitations of England, holding sessions in the counties, is based on the work of David Crook of the

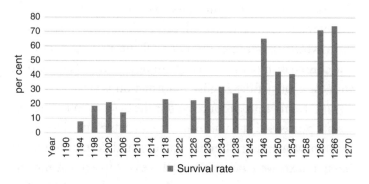

Figure 4. Survival rate of eyre rolls.

Public Record Office, who produced a guide to this material in 1982, listing not only the rolls that are still extant, but also those sessions for which there are no surviving rolls, although they must have existed. Hence it is possible to chart survival rates, and the graph in Figure 4 does that for the thirteenth century (the peak period for eyre visitations).

The graph plots the number of eyre rolls that survive as a percentage of the number of rolls we know must have been produced for any given visitation. As is clear, the survival rate increased notably over the course of the century (although not in a perfectly regular progression). Far more eyre rolls have survived from the late thirteenth century than have been lost. As David Crook commented, 'Until the reign of Edward I [1272–1307] losses are such that most attention has been directed towards trying to explain why we still have the rolls we do. From his reign onwards it is more appropriate to seek to account for the losses.' One thing that may well have influenced the survival rate is a ruling about custody of these rolls made in 1257. Prior to that date, the rolls were regarded as the private property of the judges, but in that year a royal command was issued to the treasurer and the other officials of the Exchequer, instructing them to track down the rolls that had remained in the judges' hands and place them in the treasury, and to make sure that the judges knew that henceforth this would be the procedure.

We can put another graph alongside this one. In his classic study of medieval literacy, *From Memory to Written Record*, Michael Clanchy had the inspired idea of trying to calculate the documentary output of the English government in the thirteenth century not from surviving documents but rather by working out how much sealing wax the royal chancery used. His data are the basis of the graph in Figure 5.

These two charts together thus give a clue to the production rate and survival rate for the same time, place and institution, the English royal government of the thirteenth century (although the sealing wax and the plea rolls did not emerge from the same branch of government).

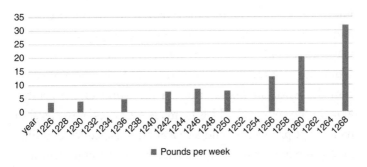

Figure 5. Pounds of wax used per week by the English royal chancery.

More was being produced, and that which was produced had a greater chance of survival.

The records of the thirteenth-century eyre, or the manuscripts of monastic libraries in Würzburg and Canterbury, are small samples, although they have the advantage of providing clear and reliable figures. Far more ambitious studies have been undertaken, however, that try to estimate total manuscript production and manuscript loss (the two figures are of course related), either for a given time and place, or even for the medieval West as a whole.

Pioneering work was done in the 1980s, when Carla Bozzolo and Ezio Ornato published a study of the manuscripts of northern France in the later Middle Ages, dealing with such issues as their number, price and the size of pages, and fully demonstrating the usefulness of quantitative analysis. Other scholars gave global estimates in passing. The great German palaeographer Bernhard Bischoff was reported to have guessed at one point that there might have been 50,000 books produced by the Carolingian scribes of the ninth century. In 1995, Wesley M. Stevens, a historian of medieval science, expressed his view that more than 1 million Latin manuscripts survive from the time before Galileo and that these represent only one-sixteenth of those that once existed (hence a loss rate of 94 per cent). The issues were put on a new footing in 1998, when Uwe Neddermeyer produced a 972-page study of the transition from the world of manuscripts to the world of the printed book, in the course of which he made estimates of the level of manuscript production and survival rates. He concluded that, for every manuscript of the fourteenth or fifteenth centuries still in existence, there would have been fourteen that no longer exist, this 1:14 ratio being remarkably close to Stevens' 1:15 (though for a shorter time span). It represents a 93 per cent loss rate. For the period from the eleventh to the fourteenth centuries Neddermeyer suggested that 12.5 per cent of the manuscript stock was lost every hundred years.

In the twenty-first century, some analysts have suggested that models used in the natural sciences for estimating uncertain populations could be applied to the question. An article in *Science* in 2005 conjectured that 'treating the manuscripts of a text as if they were fossils from an extinct population' would produce reliable results and applied this approach to Bede's scientific writings, although its assumption 'that manuscripts' destruction generally was unintentional' might be viewed as unrealistic. Another article in the same journal in 2022 started from the incontestable fact that 'historical studies of human culture are hindered by the fact that they must work with incomplete samples of material artifacts ... that still survive but do not necessarily represent the original population faithfully'. The paper sought to deal with this problem by applying methods from ecology, since 'ecologists use statistical models that account for the unseen species in samples'.

Of course, mathematical models are valuable, and can be applied to biology and ecology if certain things, for example reproduction rates, can be regarded as predictable, but there are limits to predictability. What was copied by medieval scribes was determined by cultural choices, not by natural processes. And can catastrophe be built into such models? If the extinction of the dinosaurs was indeed due to an asteroid that landed in the Gulf of Mexico, that was certainly a bolt from the blue, and it may be that the dinosaurs were doing very well before that. For English monastic libraries, the Protestant Reformation was like that asteroid strike.

One of the most ambitious attempts at quantification of medieval manuscript production and manuscript loss was undertaken by the Dutch economic statistician Eltjo Buringh. As we might expect, his approach was statistically sophisticated, but it was also based in the first instance, not on fossils or distribution of species, but on analysis of medieval library catalogues. He set himself the immense task of estimating how many medieval manuscripts survive in the modern world, calculating what the survival rate was – largely by comparing medieval catalogues and surviving manuscripts – and hence deducing the number of manuscripts produced in the Latin West in the Middle Ages. He estimated the loss rate of medieval manuscripts at 25 per cent per century, which he contrasted with Neddermeyer's loss rate of 12.5 per century. He and his co-author published preliminary conclusions on manuscript production, broken down by century, in 2009. (See the table below.)

Century	6th	7th	8th	9th	10th	11th	12th	13th	14th	15th
Manuscripts produced	13,600	10,600	43,700	201,700	135,600	212,000	768,700	1,762,000	2,747,000	4,999,100

There are some correlations here with what medievalists might guess at: the 'Carolingian Renaissance' stands out in the ninth century, while one sees exponential growth from the eleventh to the fifteenth centuries. Whether there really were 10,894,000 manuscripts produced in Latin Europe in the Middle

Ages depends on the validity both of the data fed into this table and of the statistical methods involved in the analysis. The figure is in the same range as Wesley Stevens' figure, just cited, of 16,000,000 for the period up to 1600. On the other hand, for the fifteenth century, Neddermeyer gave a figure of 2,507,500 manuscripts for the Holy Roman Empire, France, England and Italy, which would certainly imply a much lower overall figure for Latin Europe than Buringh's. One Italian reviewer commended Buringh's *'coraggio'* but described him as 'a beginner' or 'apprentice' (*apprendista*) when it comes to manuscript studies. Clearly, Buringh approached the issue as a trained statistician, but had to rely heavily on the work of others to estimate surviving manuscript numbers, to weigh up the evidence for medieval libraries, etc. In his case, Neil Ker's work on England (which has twenty entries in Buringh's index) was very important as a foundation for extrapolations (likewise, Neddermeyer had placed great weight on a census of German medieval manuscripts by Sigrid Krämer). So, those who have been bold enough to advance global figures talk of a total medieval manuscript production ranging around 10 million, while estimates of losses by various scholars are frequently around 85 to 95 per cent (85 per cent is also a tentatively suggested loss rate for documents from Fatimid Egypt, that is, from the period 969–1171). The total manuscript production of the medieval West may of course be now unknowable and irrecoverable (although there obviously is such a figure). We can, however, look at the fates and fortunes of individual medieval manuscripts, and the circumstances in which some were destroyed, while some survived – sometimes only just. The following chapter examines a famous example.

CHAPTER 4

A Narrow Escape: *Beowulf*

THERE ARE CASES OF IMPORTANT LITERARY AND historical works that survive in only one or two manuscripts. If they had suffered some accident, then our picture of the past might be altered in important ways. An interesting and unusual case is provided by the long poem that the Roman author Lucretius composed around 50 BC. In many ways it would not seem a likely candidate to be copied out by medieval monks, for it presented a completely materialist picture of the world. All that exists, says Lucretius, are atoms and the void; the atoms are infinite in number, have size and shape but no intrinsic qualities of colour, smell, etc., and their various combinations make up all that exists. The universe is infinite and contains many worlds. To say that the gods created our world is 'an act of folly'. The world will end. Mind or spirit is mortal and physical and thus cannot exist without the body. Death is the end. Religious rites and ceremonies have no effect. Hence, there is no immortal or immaterial soul, no afterlife, all is explained by the movements of matter. Yet, despite this thorough materialism, the survival of Lucretius' poem depends entirely on two manuscripts copied out in the Carolingian period, and one of them was certainly at the royal court, where it was studied and annotated by the Irish scholar Dungal. We cannot know who commissioned them or what the scribes thought about the work, but it is a remarkable fact that the survival of the longest and most eloquent expression of ancient materialist philosophy depends on the narrow thread of those two copies made in the ninth century by Christian scribes. Because the manuscript transmission was so thin, Lucretius had no direct influence on medieval thinkers. Only in 1417, when the bibliophile Poggio came across a manuscript of Lucretius' work (it no longer exists but was probably a copy of one of the two surviving Carolingian manuscripts) and made it available for copying, and, even more definitively, in 1473 when the first printed edition of the poem appeared, was this part of European cultural history truly recovered.

Another remarkable example is the historical work of Zosimus, which was probably composed in the years 498–518. By this time, the eastern Roman empire, where Zosimus lived, had been fairly thoroughly Christianized, but Zosimus was a pagan hostile to Christianity. His *New History* is one of the texts listed and commented upon by Photius (who is discussed above in Chapter 3), who calls him 'impious in matters of religion'. Zosimus blamed the decline of the Roman empire on the neglect of the old gods and suggested that the emperor Constantine had accepted the new religion because it offered him a chance to wash away the guilt for the hideous crimes he had committed. Surprisingly, Zosimus' history belongs to the 36 per cent of works listed by Photius that survive to this day – but only just. There is one manuscript, and this has several sections removed, perhaps ones that were extreme in their hostility to Christianity. The manuscript seems to have been written in Constantinople and was in the Vatican library, where it still is, by 1475. It leaves the question of how representative our surviving sources are and whether Zosimus' views were more widespread than existing evidence suggests.

The dangers of manuscript transmission and the wild chances and accidents that dictate what we know of the past are well illustrated by the epic poem *Beowulf*. *Beowulf* is the longest poem in Old English, representing more than one-tenth of the total surviving poetry from the Anglo-Saxon period, and it is also the best known. It tells the dramatic tale of the hero Beowulf, who fights and kills the monster Grendel, then confronts Grendel's mother in her underwater lair after she had come seeking revenge, and cuts her down. Fifty years later, after ruling his people well, he has to face a marauding dragon, which he kills after a fierce fight, but then dies of his wounds. The poem ends with the hero's burial and the laments of his followers. It presents a heroic, elegiac and very alien view of the world.

Beowulf has been translated dozens of times, into many languages, and has inspired films, video games and graphic novels. But this whole edifice hangs by a thread, and a study of how the poem has come down to us reveals many moments when the work could easily have disappeared for ever. It survives in one manuscript, written in England in the decades around 1000, judging by its script, but then nothing is known about it for more than 500 years. In 1563, it was in the possession of the Tudor scholar Laurence Nowell, who helpfully wrote his name and that date at the top of the first page of the poem, but there is no indication of how he had acquired it or where it had been in the Middle Ages, although one assumes it had slumbered in a monastic library until the dissolution of the monasteries under Henry VIII. Nowell was a pioneer in the study of Old English texts (he created an Old English vocabulary 187 folios in length), so it fits in well with his main scholarly interest.

Not long afterwards, the *Beowulf* manuscript somehow came into the library of Sir Robert Cotton (1571–1631), a famous book collector, whose manuscripts eventually were

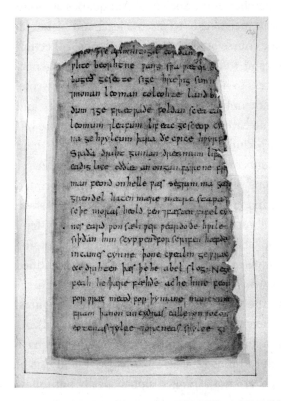

Figure 6. Beowulf manuscript, Cotton Vitellius A XV, fol.134. British Library.

to form part of the core of the British Museum (and of the British Library when this was separated from the Museum in 1973). Cotton was from the landed class, received a legal education and served several times as a Member of Parliament; he was deeply involved in politics, sometimes riskily so, in this period when the battle lines were beginning to be drawn that led eventually to civil war between king and Parliament. He was also renowned as an 'antiquary', indeed being an early member of the Society of Antiquaries, a group of gentlemen who met weekly to discuss legal and historical matters. Over the course of time, Cotton's personal collection of manuscripts came to number 800 volumes. He was generous in giving access to his library – as a contemporary wrote, he won fame 'not only from his collection of books and manuscripts of the choicest sort acquired at vast expense but also through his kindness and willingness to make them available to students of good literature and affairs of state'.

In the time of his grandson, John Cotton, a printed catalogue of the manuscripts in the collection was published. The Cottonian library had an unusual cataloguing system. Because the bookshelves were adorned with busts of the early Roman emperors, individual volumes were identified by the emperor whose bust stood above them (Julius Caesar was treated as the first emperor and two female figures, Cleopatra and the empress Faustina, were also included). As a consequence, manuscripts from the Cotton collection have shelf marks such as Julius D X or Tiberius D III, and lists of such manuscripts are not arranged alphabetically but follow the sequence of Roman emperors. The manuscript containing *Beowulf* has the shelf mark Vitellius A XV. However, in the catalogue of Cotton's manuscripts published in 1696, *Beowulf* is not even noticed among the contents of Vitellius A XV, a warning that catalogues are not always comprehensive (the catalogue entry appears to be based on Cotton's own contents list in the manuscript, which likewise omits *Beowulf*). The first mention of the poem is a few years later, in Humfrey Wanley's catalogue of Old English manuscripts in English libraries, published in 1705. Its existence was now public knowledge. Even more importantly, between the time of the 1696 catalogue and the publication of Wanley's work in 1705, the whole magnificent collection of Cotton manuscripts had been gifted by John Cotton 'for Publick Use and Advantage', secured by an Act of Parliament and the creation of a body of trustees, a very early example of a cultural treasure donated 'to the nation'.

At the time of the donation, the manuscripts were kept in Cotton House, a family property adjacent to the palace of Westminster. This building itself was purchased by the Crown in 1707, but was in a state of dilapidation, and in 1722 the library was moved to Essex House in the Strand, and then again in 1729 to Ashburnham House, Westminster, which was judged 'much more safe from fire'. Few opinions have been as wrong as that one. On the night of 23 October 1731, Ashburnham House went up in flames. The Parliamentary committee that was established to investigate this disaster reported that of 958 manuscripts housed there, 114 were 'completely destroyed', and 98 'considerably damaged'. Some treasures of the Anglo-Saxon period were lost: a version of the Anglo-Saxon Chronicle (that known as 'G' and often associated with Winchester); the sole medieval copy of

Asser's Life of King Alfred; and the sole medieval copy of the Old English poem known as *The Battle of Maldon*, describing the last stand of ealdorman Byrhtnoth against the Vikings.

Fortunately, copies of these works had been made by antiquarians and scholars in the Tudor period and later, and printed editions published before the fire. The G version of the Anglo-Saxon Chronicle had been copied by Laurence Nowell, the same man who had owned the *Beowulf* manuscript, and an edition of the text from the Cotton manuscript had been published in 1644. Asser's Life of Alfred is preserved in several sixteenth-century transcripts and editions (usually with additions) and had been published by Matthew Parker, the archbishop of Canterbury, in 1574 (he added the story of Alfred and the cakes), and by Francis Wise in 1722. Wise's edition contained a facsimile of the opening page of the Life, which has allowed informed comment on the layout and handwriting of the lost manuscript. A transcript of *The Battle of Maldon* was made less than a decade before the fire of 1731 and printed in 1726. So, although the books were lost, the texts were not. *Beowulf* was both more fortunate and less fortunate than these other Anglo-Saxon works – more fortunate in that the manuscript, although damaged, was not destroyed by the fire, less fortunate in that no transcripts had been made before 1731. If the Beowulf manuscript had been destroyed in the fire, all we would know of it would be the forty lines Wanley cited in his catalogue of 1705 and his brief and misleading summary: 'in this book, which is a remarkable example of Anglo-Saxon poetry, are described the wars that Beowulf, a certain Dane, from the royal stock of the Scyldingas, waged against the petty kings of Sweden.' No Grendel, no Grendel's mother, no dragon.

The damage to the *Beowulf* manuscript, Vitellius A XV, involved destruction of the spine and binding, so that only detached leaves survive. Hence there is no evidence of the construction of the codex, and it took some time to re-establish the proper order of the leaves. More seriously, the edges were damaged and brittle, and loss of letters at the beginning and end of lines continued long after the date of the fire itself. Some of the lost writing can be restored from a perhaps unexpected source. The story of *Beowulf* is set, not in England, but in Scandinavia, and hence drew the attention of scholars from that part of Europe. In 1787, the Icelandic scholar Grímur Jónsson Thorkelín visited London and was responsible for two transcriptions of the manuscript, one commissioned from a copyist, the other which he copied out himself. Armed with these he returned to Copenhagen, where he was based, and began work on producing a printed edition of the poem. He laboured on this for twenty years and by 1807 had a text that was ready for printing. In the meantime, the French Revolution had occurred, Napoleon had risen to power and conquered half of western Europe, and various combinations of France's enemies had formed coalitions to stop him. Britain was France's most persistent opponent and was determined to control the seas, especially in the face of Napoleon's efforts to blockade the country. Although Denmark was neutral, both sides sought to enlist it, and the British government expressed fears that the Danish fleet would be used against Britain, either as a result of an alliance of Denmark with France or through French seizure of the fleet. In response, Britain sent a strong naval expedition into Danish waters which, from 2 to 5 September 1807, bombarded Copenhagen. Especially damaging were the hundreds of rockets, which set fire to the city, reportedly destroying a thousand houses in the Danish capital. Part of the collateral damage was the manuscript of Thorkelín's edition of *Beowulf* (though not his two transcripts). The British navy had destroyed the first attempt to print the most important early English poem.

Or at least that is what Thorkelín said in the preface to his edition, when it was finally published in 1815 (along with a Latin translation). Some have doubted him, and wondered whether the British rockets were just the ideal excuse for taking twenty years not to publish an edition. And the edition, when it did come out, was subject to withering criticism. John M. Kemble, who published the next edition in 1833, did not pull his punches in discussing his predecessor: 'not five lines of Thorkelin's edition can be found in succession, in which some gross fault either in the transcript or the translation, does not betray the editor's utter ignorance of the Anglo-Saxon language.' However, whatever his scholarly failings, Thorkelín had at least been responsible for two transcripts of the poem, and, as the manuscript itself had continued to deteriorate, chiefly by flaking of the brittle margins, these were a valuable record of the original. The transcripts survive, in the Royal Library in Copenhagen, and have even been reproduced in facsimile.

Kemble's edition has been followed by many others, all of which have to rely on a combination of what can be read in Vitellius A XV, what Thorkelín's transcriptions can supply and what an educated editor might guess. There remain many disagreements in detail but hardly any in essence. This major record of early Germanic heroic verse is now a secure part of European cultural history. But it was a close thing. Surviving unread and uncopied for 500 years in some English monastic library, the manuscript passed through the turbulence of the dissolution of the monasteries and the scattering of their books, not to end up on a bonfire or to be used as a convenient wrapping for butter or fish, but to come into the hands of Tudor antiquarians and book lovers, only then to pass through the ordeal by fire of 1731, surviving but only just. It was not until 1787 that a copy was made, not until 1815 that it appeared in print, not until 1833 that there was a reputable edition. So, *Beowulf* survived. But what other works have been lost so completely that we do not even know they have been lost?

CHAPTER 5

'Away with the Learning
of the Clerks!'

A LL LIBRARIES AND ARCHIVES ARE SUBJECT TO many random threats, such as mice, floods, accidental fire, and so forth, but sometimes destruction is inflicted deliberately by humans. It is not always the case that this violence is directed specifically at the records – although there are such cases – but nevertheless the devastation that results is the same: the disappearance of written record and hence of the past. In modern times, human destructive power has increased almost beyond comprehension. Twenty-first-century generals would laugh at the firepower available to a Napoleonic army. Writing in the 1260s, Roger Bacon, the great individualist and theorist of science, foresaw that the development of military technology would reach such a point that opponents would be destroyed without any physical contact, and we are certainly at that point. Victims of destruction include not only human beings but also human records.

We will be turning to cases of the destruction of medieval manuscripts in war, but first it may be worth discussing another common threat to archives and documents, that is, an angry crowd. The poor and the non-literate might well view the mysterious parchments that were so carefully guarded by their masters as the tools of their subordination, as, in some cases, they were. During the great English revolt of

1381, the rebels in Cambridge, headed by the mayor, targeted the university and colleges, as well as the nearby priory of Barnwell. According to the Rolls of Parliament, they 'broke into the treasury of the university there, and burned the privileges and charters of the king, papal bulls, and other muniments of the said university'; they 'burned the statutes, ordinances, and many other documents of the said university'; at Corpus Christi College, 'they broke into the close of the college and the dwellings of its scholars, and seized and carried off their charters, writings, books, and other muniments'.

The king's seal on these documents was no protection:

> [They] forced the masters and scholars on threat of death to deliver and hand to them their charters and privileges and the letters patent sealed under the seal of the present king, and granted to the said university; which charters, privileges, and letters patent the said mayor, burgesses, and community burnt with a show of force in the market-place of the said town; and with knives, sticks, and other weapons they shamelessly defaced the seals of the aforesaid charters and letters patent, to the despite of our lord the king.

The smashing of the seals with knives and sticks is a particularly vivid expression of the physical hostility that these emblems of power provoked.

A famous incident is recorded after the bonfire of the ordinances and statutes of the university: 'an old woman named Margaret Sterre collected the ashes and scattered them into the wind, exclaiming, "Away with the learning of the clerks, away with it!"' It is noteworthy that she did not burn anything – she scattered the ashes. Scattering the ashes was also the final stage in obliterating the memory of heretics. In 1381, the same year as the revolt, the views of the Oxford theologian John Wycliffe, England's most famous medieval heretic, were condemned by the Church, and he withdrew to his rural parsonage, dying there two years later. But the ecclesiastical authorities continued to pursue him after death, and in 1428 his bones were dug up and burned, and the ashes scattered in a nearby river, 'so that henceforth no remains or trace can appear of him, whose memory is to be obliterated'. When Margaret Sterre threw handfuls of ashes into the chilly Cambridge air, it may be that she was attempting a similar final and irrevocable gesture of annihilation, ensuring 'the learning of the clerks' would never plague her again. The law generated documents. The poor experienced these documents as chains. It was therefore natural for them to seek to destroy documents when they had the chance – 'away with the learning of the clerks!'

Lawyers as well as legal documents were a target. In London in 1381, the rebels attacked the Inns of Court, where lawyers were trained: 'they broke open the chests that they found in the church or in the students' rooms and with their axes chopped up any books they could find, whether they were ecclesiastical, or charters and muniments in the students' chests, and fed them to the fire.' Lawyers and law students were hunted down. According to one account, the rebels 'had it cried throughout the city that all men of law, and all those of the chancery and Exchequer, and all who knew how to write a brief or a letter, should be beheaded wherever they might be found'.

The chronicler Thomas Walsingham gives a heightened account of the rebels' hostility to the very ability to read or write:

> They forced the teachers in the schools of grammar to
> swear that they would never in future teach that skill to the
> young. What more did they do? They eagerly gave old
> records to the flames and, to ensure that henceforth no one
> should be found who knew how to preserve in memory
> either the old ones or new ones, such they killed. It was
> dangerous to be known as a cleric but much more
> dangerous if you were found with an inkwell – such people
> scarcely or never escaped their hands.

Documents, seals, inkwells – all were seen as hated instruments of oppression. It is an attitude that was memorably parodied in Shakespeare's *Henry VI, Part ii*, act 4, scene 2, which is set during Jack Cade's rebellion of 1450, a similar event to that of 1381, though on a far smaller scale. In Shakespeare's play, Cade's follower, Dick the Butcher, suggests, 'The first thing we do, let's kill all the lawyers,' to which Cade responds,

> Nay, that I mean to do. Is not this a lamentable thing, that of
> the skin of an innocent lamb should be made parchment?
> that parchment, being scribbled o'er, should undo a man?
> Some say the bee stings, but I say 'tis the bee's wax; for I did
> but seal once to a thing, and I was never mine own man since.

Later, the rebels bring a charge against a clerk – 'he can write and read' – and Cade condemns him to be hanged 'with his pen and inkhorn about his neck'. In scene 4 of the same act,

Cade accuses Lord Say: 'Thou hast most traitorously cor-
rupted the youth of the realm in erecting a grammar
school . . . thou hast caused printing to be used, and, contrary
to the king his crown and dignity, thou hast built a papermill.'
The last two of these indictments are clearly anachronistic,
but they help to build up a picture of a recalcitrant lower class
instinctively suspicious of the whole machinery of literacy.

The events in Cambridge and London during the
revolt of summer 1381 are recorded in detail in contemporary
chronicles and government records. In the rural localities, the
first target of peasant rebels in that year was often the manorial court rolls that recorded their obligations and status.
Writing of the revolt, the historian of the medieval English
peasantry Christopher Dyer concluded 'the burning of court
rolls was one of the most widespread expressions of rural
rebellion', and he could identify over a hundred such incidents. This was one of the things that was remembered about
the rising – the record of a manor court held at Moze in Essex
on 23 September, after the suppression of the rising, is headed,
'The first court after the revolt and the burning of the rolls'.

Attacks on written records during popular uprisings
can be found throughout the Middle Ages, from 579, when the
people of Limoges, angered by new and heavier taxation,
seized the tax registers from the hands of a royal official and
burned them, to 1308, when peasants invaded Parma, broke
open the archives and tore up the documents, throwing them
out of the window and 'created great clouds of torn charters
that entirely covered the square below. And in this way these
peasants cancelled their fines and released themselves from
what they owed.'

Books and documents were also a target in 1525 during the so-called Peasants' War in Germany, when large bands of rural tenants – but also many members of other classes – assembled in arms and attacked monasteries and castles throughout central and southern Germany. The risings took place within ten years of Luther's famous stand against the practice of indulgences in 1517, traditionally regarded as the beginning of the Protestant Reformation, and there is evidence that some of the insurgents were inspired by religious motives, but they were also inspired by class hatred. Luther quickly and dramatically distanced himself from them. As always, he went into print, publishing *Against the Murderous, Thieving Hordes of Peasants* in May 1525.

The documents of the lords and rich churches were a prominent target of the rebellious peasants. When they assailed the margrave of Baden's castle of Rötteln near Basel, the only thing they destroyed was the vault in which the documents and estate records were stored. In April 1525, after the peasants gained entry to the town of Heilbronn, they plundered the buildings of the Teutonic Knights, who owned extensive estates in the region, and scattered the accounts and papers of the Order, throwing them into a nearby stream. Many of the peasants involved were rural tenants of the Knights. When the insurgents came to the Cistercian abbey of Herrenalb in the Black Forest, they tore up the documents of the abbey and decorated their hats with the parchment scraps, giving the event a semi-carnival atmosphere (they often marched with pipes and drums).

Monasteries sometimes tried to get their archives off to safe sites. The Benedictines of Schwarzach took some of their documents to Strasbourg, 30 km south, for safekeeping, but those documents that remained at the abbey and all the books were torn up and burned. The abbot of Langheim, which is a little distance north of Bamberg, sent off 'the relics, privileges and other treasures' of the abbey to the bishop of Bamberg's castle at Altenburg, high above the city. Here they survived the Peasants' War undamaged. However, when the bishop himself left Bamberg to seek safety in the castle at Altenburg, this was a signal for the insurgents to fall on the city, plundering and

> ripping up books, registers, letters and other things, especially at the treasury office, where there were many old books, court records, registers and many other things, and these were all hacked up and torn to pieces and scattered around the citadel, with the result that the citadel was covered with torn books and letters, so that people had to walk on them in every street.

The German lower classes had practical reasons for destroying legal documentation. Books and libraries were a different matter. The insurgents' destruction of service books in monastic churches or aristocratic chapels may well have had a religious impulse behind it, but there were other motives, including economic ones, for plundering books. Gilded and bejewelled book covers were targets, for obvious reasons, but even books without such precious (and detachable) items could have value, and merchants seem to have followed the peasant bands in order to purchase books, as well as much else – though it appears there was a glut on the market, since one of the insurgents who plundered the rich library at

Ellwangen said that he had later sold twelve volumes for a penny.

But the destruction of books had meaning in itself. When the peasants used the monastic books and documents as fuel for the stove, or as stepping stones over muddy ground, this was not a practical matter but a symbolic gesture. The scholar and librarian Karl Schottenloher, who, in 1909, published an article on the fate of books and libraries during the Peasants' War, wrote 'in the written and printed word the insurgents saw a source of all their oppressions and a privilege of the propertied classes . . . the peasants and the poor saw in books evidence of an alien and oppressive culture'. This feeling was what lay behind the furious destruction of books and documents. A Utopian scheme for a peasant republic that was drawn up in the aftermath of the failure of the rising, perhaps as a consolation of some kind, specified that in this new ideal world 'the Word of God should be preached truly and faithfully, and all sophistry and legalism eradicated and such books burned'.

In 1701, a similar anger was directed against the state archives of the kingdom of Naples stored in the Castel Capuano, which had been built originally as a royal palace but since the sixteenth century had housed the Hall of Justice, including prisons. These disturbances did not start with the rage and resentment of the common people, but with a political division among the ruling class, which the commoners then took advantage of. The War of the Spanish Succession, which was triggered by the death of Charles II of Spain in 1700, was a dynastic struggle between adherents of the Habsburg and Bourbon dynasties, and this conflict extended to the kingdom of Naples, part of the Spanish domains. In 1700, Naples recognized the succession of the Bourbon, Philip V of Spain, but the following year a pro-Habsburg conspiracy was formed, which planned a rising for the night of 22–3 September 1701. The aristocratic leaders of this rising had some initial success and managed to enter the Castel Capuano. At this point, a crowd of Neapolitans who had gathered in their wake seized their opportunity and rushed in after them.

> They began to burn all the documents indiscriminately and to destroy all the archives. It was amazing to see so many people with such rage, who in a short time set on fire so many papers and documents, books and trial records, that perhaps a thousand carts could not have carried, removing all the volumes of the archive from more than seven centuries.

The crowd stripped the rooms of every piece of wood to fuel 'more than fifteen' bonfires.

> With a rage never seen, they threw so many documents and books into the courtyard, casting them down from every window . . . the fires burned for three or more days, one of them leaving a deposit of ash three hands deep, precisely where the documents of the criminal archive were kept. More damage was done in a day and a half than could have been done by a thousand soldiers in a week.

It is clearly not accidental that the fiercest fire was where the criminal records were kept.

The same hatred of these oppressive documents is seen in the French Revolution, during the so-called 'Great

Fear' in the summer of 1789. This uprising of the French peasantry against their aristocratic landlords had as a special target the registers and title deeds housed in the châteaux of the nobles. Early reports of the unrest mentioned 'daily talk of attacking the nobility, or setting fire to their châteaux in order to burn all their title deeds'; rebels later 'demanded their title deeds'; in Normandy 'they were going to burn the charter collection at La Coulonche [Orne] and if they did not find it then they would burn the château'; a police officer at Chalon-sur-Saône considered that 'they seem to have gathered by common consent with the intention of laying waste châteaux and houses and freeing themselves from their rents by burning their charters.' There are certainly numerous cases during this 'Great Fear' where châteaux were burned with no mention of archives or deeds, but there are also clear instances where the surrender of the deeds was the goal and the châteaux were left intact.

Attacks on archives and documents, from the Middle Ages to the 1780s, often had practical aims – to destroy written records that were unfavourable to the crowds who burned them, unfavourable either because they were a record of harsh terms and inferior status or, in the case of court documents, because they preserved a criminal record. Likewise, attacks on the records of Jewish lending, which were often led by the debtors, obviously had the similarly practical goal of destroy-ing the evidence of the debt – in 1190, for example, after a ferocious massacre of the Jews of York, the Christian mob 'immediately went to the cathedral, and with great violence seized from the terrified custodians the records of debt that the Jewish moneylenders had deposited there, and to free

themselves and others, destroyed those instruments of pro-
fane greed by fire in the middle of the church'. But there was
always also a symbolic side to these events. There was clearly
more than simple practical calculation at work in instances
where the destruction was indiscriminate: it is hard to believe
that the Neapolitans throwing 'the volumes of the archive
from more than seven centuries' onto bonfires were thinking
in narrowly pragmatic terms. There was a more general hostility to documents here. When Margaret Sterre cast the ashes
of the burned parchments to the winds, nothing practical was
gained beyond what the burning of the documents had
already achieved – she was engaged in a triumphant gesture.
And it is worth reflecting on what she reportedly called out,
usually translated as 'Away with the learning of the clerks,
away with it!' Margaret must have spoken in English, but her
actions and words were recorded in Latin, the learned language of the chronicler, and the Latin word translated here as
'learning' (*peritia*) can equally mean 'expertise, special skill';
and what was that 'special skill' of the clerks that she hated
and perhaps feared? Quite simply, writing.

CHAPTER 6

Strasbourg, 24 August 1870:
The Garden of Delights

O<small>N 19 JULY 1870 FRANCE DECLARED WAR ON PRUSSIA</small> (this was a time when states still officially declared war). The immediate cause was relatively insignificant, a dispute about whether a relative of the king of Prussia could become king of Spain, but the two countries had a long history of conflict: in 1806 Napoleon had won several decisive victories against Prussian armies and occupied Berlin, the Prussian capital, and the following year imposed a peace treaty that reduced the kingdom to almost half its previous size. Seven years later, in 1814, the Prussians had their revenge and marched into Paris with their allies, then, after Napoleon's remarkable last gamble, played a decisive part in the allied victory and the final defeat of the French at Waterloo on 18 June 1815. The allied troops remained in France until 1818 to ensure payment of reparations. All this would be familiar at a personal level to the sovereigns of Prussia and France in 1870: as a young man King Wilhelm I had fought at Waterloo, while the emperor of the French, Napoleon III, was a nephew of Napoleon.

In the war, Prussia was supported by the south German states of Bavaria, Baden and Württemberg. The frontier between France and the German states consisted of two stretches of about 100 miles (160 kilometres), one following the course of the Rhine, the other, going west from the

Rhine, a land frontier. The German strategy was to invade France along this land frontier. Three armies advanced and, within two months, won six battles, captured Napoleon III and began the siege of Paris. Meanwhile, from 15 August to 27 September, the major French city of Strasbourg was bombarded by encircling German troops. Strasbourg lay on the Rhine and was a border city. It had been German until 1681, when Louis XIV annexed it. After the French surrender at the official end of the war in 1871, it became a German city once more, then was French again in 1919, and under German occupation and administration from 1940 to 1944. Like many other cities, it has more than one name (Strasbourg, Straßburg), a sure mark of a history of political complexity (compare Lviv/Lvov/Lemberg; Derry/Londonderry, etc.).

During the bombardment of 1870, civilian casualties were heavy, and the city was damaged by fire and explosion.

Figure 7. Strasbourg, 1870. Royal Geographical Society / Getty Images.

At the height of the attack, 4,000 shells a night landed in the city centre. France had not experienced enemy troops on its soil since 1818, and contemporaries were shocked by this assault on a large civilian population. One site that suffered very badly was the complex of buildings housed in the former Dominican convent (known as the Temple-Neuf), which included the Protestant church and high school, along with their libraries and the town library. Around 8:30 p.m. on 24 August 1870, as a result of a heavy bombardment, these libraries, with their thousands of books and manuscripts, went up in flames. The burning of the libraries, it has been said, 'was felt by the whole learned world as an irreparable catastrophe'. Many of the manuscripts and older books had come into the Strasbourg library when the religious houses were nationalized at the time of the French Revolution, so they included medieval manuscripts. Their greatest treasure was a unique illustrated encyclopaedia of the late twelfth century known as *The Garden of Delights* (*Hortus deliciarum*).

The Garden of Delights was a product of the enthusiasm and initiative of Herrad, abbess of Hohenburg (Mont Sainte-Odile), a convent perched on a height in the Vosges mountains about 20 miles (30 kilometres) south-west of Strasbourg. In its original state, when completed around 1190, *The Garden of Delights*, a substantial volume of about 20 inches by 14 inches (50 centimetres by 36 centimetres), had 342 folios, and contained excerpts from 1,160 Latin texts, ranging from the Old Testament to the latest theological writings from Paris, and including 66 sermons and 55 poems, some of them with musical notation. But the glory of *The Garden of Delights* was not its text, which was mainly an assemblage of well-known sources, but its pictures. It contained 346 illustrations, which started with the fall of Lucifer (Satan) and the creation of the world, then proceeded through the biblical stories of the Garden of Eden, the Fall, Noah, Abraham, Moses, Samson and the prophets, before turning to the New Testament: the Life of Christ, Pentecost, the acts of the apostles, Paul, and, looking to the future, the coming of Antichrist, Heaven and Hell. But interspersed in this chronological sequence are other images, such as the muses, the Seven Liberal Arts, Ulysses and the sirens, and two pictures specifically related to the convent of Hohenburg, to which we will return.

This remarkable book is first mentioned, centuries after its creation, by Jerome (Hieronymus) Gebwiler, who attests that it was still at the convent of Hohenburg in 1521: 'a beautiful big Latin book, called *The Garden of Delights*'. He also says that abbess Herrad was a member of the von Landsberg family, though he gives no reason for this claim. The Landsbergs were a family of knightly status in Alsace, the region in which Strasbourg is situated, and Herrad is often called 'Herrad von Landsberg' in scholarly and general literature to this day. Much later, the family claimed ownership of the book, but were only successful in obtaining it for a short time. At some point, it is not known how, the manuscript of *The Garden of Delights* came into the possession of the Carthusian monks of Molsheim, 14 miles (22 kilometres) west of Strasbourg, and, when all religious bodies in France were dissolved in 1790, it passed to the library of the département, which subsequently became the municipal library of Strasbourg. Hence its vulnerability to German

shelling in 1870, when 'one of the most ambitious and splendid manuscripts of the middle ages' was 'irretrievably
destroyed'.

Knowledge of *The Garden of Delights* did not dis-
appear forever in 1870, when it was incinerated, because
several generations of scholars had previously made the effort
to describe it and make copies of its illustrations. The earliest
was Christian Moritz Engelhardt (1775–1858), from a
Protestant merchant family in Strasbourg. Engelhardt was
fascinated by the Middle Ages and by the Alps, making him
the model early Romantic (he ended up as Strasbourg's police
chief, which is perhaps less romantic). He published on both
subjects, reporting his wanderings in the mountains and also
pioneering the publication of images from medieval manuscripts. In 1812 he made tracings of several images from *The
Garden of Delights* and, in 1818, published a book about the
manuscript with twelve full-page plates engraved from his
tracings, some copies having the images hand-coloured. The
book has been claimed as 'one of the earliest on any medieval
manuscript'. Engelhardt continued to make drawings from
the manuscript in the 1830s.

The next important figure in this story is the memorably named Count Bastard. Auguste de Bastard d'Estang
(1792–1883) was born in Gascony, a younger son of a minor
aristocratic family, and made his way through military service, being wounded and captured at the battle of Leipzig in
1813. After the defeat of Napoleon, he continued in the army
until 1849, serving as captain of the royal guard under the
restored Bourbon kings, but he combined military service
with his study of medieval manuscripts, especially the

illustrated ones. His contribution in this field was great. In 1864, an admirer wrote, 'It is you who has galvanized all these glorious remains of the past and, at your voice, the whole Middle Ages rises again in its splendour and magnificence.'

Bastard was so committed to this project that he himself qualified as a lithographer, to produce coloured reproductions of medieval images. Lithography, which had been invented in Germany in the 1790s, is a complex process. A drawing is made on a flat polished stone with a special greasy ink. The stone is then treated chemically, using gum arabic, in such a way that the lines of the drawing are fixed. When the whole stone is inked, the ink is repelled from the blank areas. A sheet of paper is laid on top of the stone and put into a press. The result is a reverse image of what was drawn. To produce coloured lithographs, several stones must be prepared with different coloured inks. The sheet of paper then has to be aligned on each successively to obtain a full colour reproduction. Alternatively, the black-and-white image may be hand coloured, as was the case with some of Bastard's work.

Bastard's major project, *Manuscript Paintings and Decoration* (*Peintures et ornements des manuscrits*), which was initiated in 1834 with French government support, involved the publication of reproductions of medieval manuscript paintings and was issued in instalments over many years, eventually totalling 261 plates. Forty-eight plates were displayed at the Great Exhibition in London in 1851. Bastard turned his attention to *The Garden of Delights* around 1840 and was able to have the manuscript sent from Strasbourg to Paris so that he could study it (the free-and-easy treatment of medieval manuscripts in the eighteenth and nineteenth centuries never ceases to freeze the blood of modern medievalists). He commissioned Wilhelm Stengel to go carefully through the manuscript, to describe it, and make extensive notes and sketches. Eleven plates of illustrations were prepared. All this preparatory material is now in the National Library of France.

After the destruction of the manuscript in 1870, two canons of Strasbourg cathedral, Alexandre Straub and Gustave Keller, undertook to 'gather up the fragments' and publish any copies made before the disaster. They had access not only to the published plates of Engelhardt and Bastard but also to many unpublished drawings and tracings made by these and other scholars. The result, published in instalments and completed in 1899, was a volume with an explanatory text and 113 plates of illustrations, reproduced by 'heliography', a process of engraving in which a specially prepared plate is acted upon chemically by exposure to light. Straub and Keller's was the standard work on *The Garden of Delights* until 1979. In that year there appeared two volumes, published by the Warburg Institute of London and Brill of Leiden, that offered as complete a reconstruction of the original manuscript as, one imagines, will ever be possible. It was edited by Rosalie Green (1917–2012), at the time director of the Index of Christian Art at Princeton University (now known as the Index of Medieval Art), and since the Index was dedicated to amassing information about, and photographs of, images of all kinds from the Middle Ages (as it still is), this was an ideal background.

Volume I contained a 'reconstruction' of the manuscript of *The Garden of Delights* at two-thirds scale. All available text and images, as preserved by the notes and drawings of the nineteenth-century scholars who had studied the manuscript before its destruction, were arranged in what was considered the original order. Sometimes, all that was known about a particular page would be the subject of the text, but not the text itself, or just a fragment of an image. Whatever there was, was reproduced and put in place. When coloured images were available, these were printed in colour. Volume II contained expert commentary on the history of the manuscript, the paintings, the script and other important aspects of *The Garden of Delights*, as well as 360 images showing parallels and possible sources for the illustrations in Herrad's book.

All this reconstructive work enables us to form a good general idea of the nature of *The Garden of Delights*. Its author, its title and its intended audience are given at the beginning of the book. Herrad salutes the community in Latin verse: 'Hail company of virgins of Hohenburg, white as a lily, loving the Son of God. The most devoted Herrad, your most faithful mother and little handmaid, sings you songs.' The title is spelled out: 'Here begins *The Garden of Delights*, in which the little band of young women may be constantly delighted by the flowers of scripture gathered here.' In this garden, Herrad was a little bee: 'I have compiled this book, inspired by God, like a little bee, and I have assembled it, as it were, into one sweet honeycomb, out of love for you.' The image of an anthology as a garden or a collection of flowers is widespread and ancient (the word 'anthology' comes from the Greek for a 'gathering of flowers'). An illustrated encyclopaedia that is in some ways like *The Garden of Delights* was produced by Lambert of Saint-Omer in the years 1090–1120 and is titled the *Liber floridus*, 'the flowery book' (Lambert's original manuscript survives in Ghent University Library, having avoided destruction in two world wars). Many literary works of the Middle Ages were compilations of earlier texts. Moreover, the sources from which encyclopaedias were compiled might themselves be collections of texts from elsewhere – medieval writers often copied earlier writers, who themselves were often copying yet earlier writers. In such cases a chain can be traced, perhaps going back to the early Christian or ancient world. A simple example can illustrate this.

On folio 9 of *The Garden of Delights*, we read: 'The sun becomes hotter from the great motion of its revolution, since it is a fiery body. Because the sun is higher than the moon and yet it still seems larger than the moon to us, if the sun were to come close to us, it would appear much larger than the moon.' This is part of a section on the creation of the world. The 'revolution' of the sun does not mean it turns on its axis, but that it rotates around the earth, while the discussion of the size of the sun and moon makes clear the distinction between size as perceived by us and absolute size. Not a word of all this is an original formulation of Herrad's. Here she was relying, as in other places, on an encyclopaedia that had been composed in Germany almost two centuries earlier, the so-called 'Summary of Henry' (*Summarium Heinrici*) – no one knows who Henry was – dating to about 1020. But neither are the words Henry's. He was quoting (with some rearrangement) what had been written by Isidore, bishop of Seville, author of the enormously influential *Etymologies*, a mammoth encyclopaedia organized around words, lists and verbal categories that Isidore had drawn up in the period 610–636. It became one of the most common handbooks of general knowledge of the Middle Ages. So, down through the centuries, encyclopaedias drew on encyclopaedias (perhaps like today), and religious women in a German convent in the 1180s could read about the nature of the universe in the words of a Spanish bishop who wrote 550 years earlier.

A thorough reading of the texts in *The Garden of Delights* and a study of its pictures would constitute a superb introduction to the Christian culture of the medieval West, its biblical foundations, its beliefs about cosmography and geography, its educational programme, its conception of the sacraments and the virtues and vices, and much more. There are some passages which contain social comment. In a dialogue between an unnamed pupil and an unnamed teacher, the pupil asks the teacher for his views on different social groupings:

> PUPIL: What do you think of knights?
>
> TEACHER: Little good. They live from plunder, they clothe themselves from looting, this is how they purchase their possessions, this is how they pay for their fiefs. It is said of them, 'their days were consumed in vanity', hence 'the wrath of God will come upon them'.
>
> PUPIL: What hope have merchants?
>
> TEACHER: Little. For they acquire almost all they have through fraud, perjury, theft and dishonest gains …
>
> PUPIL: Do jesters have any hope?
>
> TEACHER: None. In all they do, they are ministers of Satan. Of them it is said, 'they did not know God', so 'God despised them' … the mockers will be mocked.

It is easy to imagine Herrad's community of religious women listening to this with a strong sense of how right the teacher was, and perhaps with a frisson of pleasant horror. It should be pointed out, however, that elsewhere in the book a quite different view of knights is expressed: 'Knights are an arm of the Church, who ought to defend it from enemies. It is fitting for them to help the oppressed, to restrain themselves from looting and fornication, to resist those who are disobedient to the priests.' The coexistence of these two views of knights is to be explained in part because any huge anthology of texts is likely to contain contradictory views and statements, but also because this period, the twelfth century, really was a time of changing views about knighthood. The brutal horse-warriors of the tenth and eleventh centuries were gradually being transformed into the chivalric heroes of the later Middle Ages. Part of this process was the crusade, which gave knights a spiritually sanctioned function. The crusading Orders, like the Templars, were, in St Bernard's words, a 'New Knighthood'. The texts in *The Garden of Delights* reflect this transformational and contradictory process, as condemnation was replaced by exhortation and idealization.

But the book conveyed the Christian version of human history in pictures as well as in words. Particularly impressive are the dramatic full-page coloured illustrations. One shows the Seven Liberal Arts (so-called because they were the proper studies of the free man – *liber* – as distinct from the mechanical arts such as agriculture, weaving and carpentry). They comprised: Grammar; Rhetoric; Logic; Arithmetic; Astronomy; Music; Geometry. In the book each is personified as a lady in a full-length gown, with the extravagant long sleeves of the period, holding an object symbolic of the art they represent: Grammar has a book and a bundle of birch twigs (for beating students who did not work hard enough), Music a harp, lute and organistrum (a kind of hurdy-gurdy), Geometry has a measuring rod and a pair of compasses, and so on. These ladies are arranged in a circle around a smaller circle in the middle of the page, in which we see Socrates and Plato busily writing at their desks beneath the enthroned female figure of Philosophy. At the foot of the page there is a warning: we see four male figures, seated and writing away, but this time inspired by evil spirits who hover at their ear. These are 'poets or magicians', and they are writing 'magic and poetry, that is, false fables'. The philosophy of Socrates and Plato could be integrated into the Christian world, but the ancient pagan poets were more suspect.

Two pictures – the Wheel of Fortune and the Ladder of Virtues – illustrate the precariousness of human life. The former was an ancient and common symbol of the uncertainties of our existence, a reminder of how you might be on top one minute and cast down to the depths the next. The wheel is turned by Fortuna, a crowned female figure seated on a throne, who operates a long-handled crank to move the wheel around. Perched on the top of the wheel is a king in his glory, but his position is shaky, for just to his right, as the wheel turns, another king is sliding down, desperately holding on, although his crown is slipping, while below him is a third king, completely upside down, whose crown has fallen off his head. Meanwhile, as the wheel brings down these kings, on the other side it brings up other figures, with their ambitious eyes fixed on the crowned king at the top. If you are at the top, you will not stay there long, and there are always rivals eager to take your place. The other picture shows the Ladder of Virtues stretching from earth, where the devil lies in wait in the form of a dragon, to heaven, where God's hand holds out the crown of life. The two sides of the ladder are love of God and love of one's neighbour, and it has fifteen rungs, each standing for a virtue – patience, benevolence and so forth – but it is perilously easy to fall off the ladder, however holy your life may appear. Various types are depicted tumbling down from the rungs: at the bottom, a knight and a lay woman represent lay people, who are given to vices like fornication, avarice and pride, and rarely turn their eyes to the crown of life; above them we see a false nun being seduced by a priest, a cleric who is given to drinking and lechery, and a monk who treasures property and wealth; towards the top of the ladder are hermits, supposedly the spiritual elite, but these think more about their garden than about prayer. They are all slipping or falling headlong.

If you fell off the ladder for good, Hell awaited you. In *The Garden of Delights*, Hell is represented in a dramatic full-page picture: at the right, at the left and at the top of the page, there is a framework of grey rock, punctuated by the mouths of caves, from which emerge flames and naked human beings. This rocky framework encloses four levels, each filled with fire and populated by devils, who are depicted as naked, muscular, dark-grey figures, whose spiky hair grows straight up from their head. Everywhere humans are being tormented – by snakes and toads, by being hung upside-down, by devils with pitchforks. Most are naked, although there are two ladies in

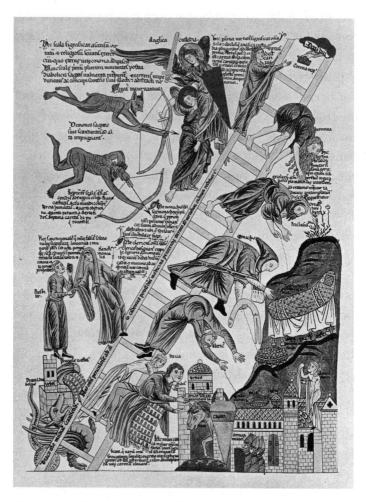

Figure 8. The *Hortus deliciarum* of Herrad of Hohenbourg – fol. 215v, p. 352, plate 124. *The Hortus deliciarum of Herrad of Hohenbourg*, ed. Rosalie Green et al. (2 vols., London, 1979), facsimile volume. © The Warburg Institute.

long dresses suffering, perhaps for their concern with fashion. On the third level down, two giant cauldrons stand on the flames, one full of Jews, the other of armoured knights. The former are shown with the distinctive Jewish pointed hat, the latter with coats of mail and helmets with nose-guards, but the cauldrons are also labelled to remove any doubt. Devils are shown bringing another Jew and another knight to toss into the cauldrons. At the bottom of Hell sits the enormous, grinning figure of 'Lucifer or Satan', with Antichrist in his lap. Seventeen devils and almost fifty humans are shown in the scene. It is all very crowded, very claustrophobic, very literal. As Thomas Bilson, bishop of Winchester, remarked in a sermon of 1599, 'The fire of hell they will say is metaphorical; they that go thither shall find it no metaphor.' Medieval theologians taught that the saved in heaven would be able to see the damned being tormented in hell, and through this picture Herrad's community had an anticipation of that pleasure.

In the preface of *The Garden of Delights* Herrad had addressed her 'little band of young women'. Right at the end of the volume, there are two full-page illustrations that return the focus from the wider Christian vision found in the body of the book back to the specific community of the Hohenburg, Herrad's community. Like many religious establishments, the nuns of Hohenburg looked back to a semi-legendary founder of the early Middle Ages. In their case, this was St Odilia or Odile (which is why Hohenburg is also known as Mont Sainte-Odile). While there is evidence that there was a community of religious women on the Hohenburg from at least the time of Charlemagne (768–814), there is no account of Odilia until the tenth century. At that time, a Life of St Odilia

Figure 9. The *Hortus deliciarum* of Herrad of Hohenbourg – fol. 255, p. 438, plate 146. *The Hortus deliciarum of Herrad of Hohenbourg*, ed. Rosalie Green et al. (2 vols., London, 1979), facsimile volume. © The Warburg Institute.

was written, which eventually became a widespread text, surviving in dozens of manuscripts across Germany and Italy, and even making its way to Worcester by the twelfth century, where the chronicler John of Worcester incorporated it into his history, though mistakenly placing Odilia in his own time, the 1130s.

This tenth-century account of Odilia tells of an illustrious duke in the time of King Childerich II (662–75) who decides to found a monastery on the Hohenburg. Meanwhile, his wife gives birth to a baby girl who is born blind. The duke is ashamed and commands that the baby be killed, but the mother manages to smuggle her away to the care of an old family retainer, who later takes the child to a nunnery. Here she is baptized and named Odilia by a visiting bishop and immediately recovers her sight. She grows up and pursues the religious life in the convent, and then writes to her brother, who is still at the court of the duke their father, and her brother summons her to return, in defiance of their father's wishes. The duke is overcome with rage and strikes his son, killing him, but is immediately smitten with remorse. He gives the convent of Hohenburg to his daughter and soon thereafter dies. She learns that he is suffering in the afterlife for his sins and secures his release through prayer. She raises the number of sisters to 130, builds a hospice at the bottom of the mountain for the poor and pilgrims, and experiences many miraculous events before dying on 13 December, which would be celebrated as her feast-day.

So now Odilia had everything a medieval saint needed: a story of her life, miracles, a feast-day, a community dedicated to her memory. This was the saintly founding figure

Herrad's community would have known. Her image, and that of her father the duke, were carved on a pillar in their convent at Hohenburg. And her story appears on folio 322v of *The Garden of Delights*. In the upper part of the page, we see St Odilia, with a halo, standing next to John the Baptist, who is captioned 'St John the Baptist, whom St Odilia loved especially, more than other saints'. They face Christ, who is centrally placed, looking outwards. Next to him are the Virgin Mary and St Peter, and all three of them are holding or touching a long rod, which is being proffered by the kneeling figure of the duke – handing over a rod was a common symbolic act signifying the transfer of property. The adjacent text explains that the duke, here called 'Eticho or Adalricus' and described as a saint, although he has no halo, is handing over to Christ, St Mary and St Peter the monastery he has founded in Hohenburg. In the lower half of this page there are two separate images. One shows the duke, seated, handing a huge key to St Odilia, 'first abbess of Hohenburg', who stands in front of her community of religious women. The other image whisks us forwards 500 years and shows Rilinda, who was abbess immediately before Herrad and is credited with restoring and reforming Hohenburg. The past and the present are woven together, the founding figure of ancient days and the reforming abbess the sisters might well remember.

When the book was open, this illustrated page with Odilia and Rilinda would be visible at the same time as the next one, folio 323, containing the last image in the book. This is very unusual. It has a heading: 'The religious congregation in the time of abbesses Rilinda and Herrad, joined in charity in the service of God in Hohenburg.' It shows sixty members

Figure 10. The *Hortus deliciarum* of Herrad of Hohenbourg – fols. 322v–323, pp. 345–6, plates 153–4. *The Hortus deliciarum of Herrad of Hohenbourg*, ed. Rosalie Green et al. (2 vols., London, 1979), facsimile volume. © The Warburg Institute.

of the Hohenbourg community, all of the same size, head and shoulders depicted only, and identical general appearance,

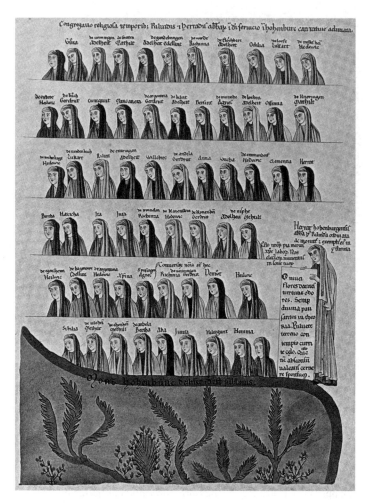

Figure 10. (cont.)

presided over by the much larger, full-length figure of Herrad. They gaze to their right, so appear to be contemplating Odilia and Rilinda on the opposite page. And, although they are

90

indistinguishable from each other visually, they are all named –
so, if the book was exhibited to them, the last thing the sisters
would see would be themselves and their names.

With only six exceptions, the sisters bear traditional
Germanic aristocratic names: one is called Odilia, like the first
abbess, one is called Herrad, like the present abbess; there are
five cases each of Hedwig, Matilda and Gertrude, and no
fewer than seven of Adelheid. The six exceptions are Agnes,
Anna, Christina, Clementia, Margaret and Sybil. Apart from
Sybil, these are the names of Christian saints, mostly early
martyrs, though Anna is the mother of the Virgin Mary, and
represent the beginning of a trend that was to strengthen in
following centuries, as such names multiply, diminishing the
dominance of traditional Germanic names. Sybil is different,
being neither an old Germanic name nor the name of a
Christian saint. In origin it is Greek and most famously refers
to an ancient prophetess, who, in the Christian view, pre-
dicted the coming of Christ. The name seems to have first
come to the West in Italy, then spread to the Normans and
crusaders (there was a Queen Sybil of Jerusalem at just the
time *The Garden of Delights* was being created). It is entirely
possible that the Sybil in the book can be identified individu-
ally. The German ruler at this time, Henry VI, claimed the
kingdom of Sicily (southern Italy) in right of his wife, and in
1194 conquered it, displacing the royal family. Sybil, the queen
mother, was sent to confinement in the Hohenburg (although
she eventually made her escape to France). If the woman
pictured in *The Garden of Delights* is indeed she, and Sybil
was at this time a very rare name in the German-speaking
world, then this helps date the work. As well as first names,

more than half of the members of the community (35) have surnames, all of them in the form 'of' plus a place name, such as Matilda of Schneidheim, Hedwig of Treuchtlingen, Edellint of Hagenau. The Latin for 'of' is *de*, the German *von*. German surnames in *von* came to be associated with the aristocracy but can also simply indicate the place where one was from. What Hedwig von Treuchtlingen thought of her fellow nuns without surnames (or they of her) we can only guess.

The body of the text of *The Garden of Delights* is in Latin, the usual language of the medieval western Church, but on many occasions the German equivalent of a Latin word is inserted either between the lines or in the margin (these are termed 'glosses'). There are in fact 1,250 German glosses and, as one might expect, modern philologists and linguists have been very interested in this large sample of medieval German vocabulary. Presumably many of the nuns were much more at home with German, their mother tongue, than with Latin, a learned language. The glosses sometimes suggest something more than linguistic information. When we read the Latin phrase *publica vel regia via*, which means, literally, 'a public or royal way/road', we think of authority, rule, the echoes of the Roman empire. The German gloss at this point is *heristraze*, meaning 'army road'. We think instead of a large body of armed men on their way to a violent encounter. The translation of the Latin *Britannia* (Britain) with the German *Engillant* (England) reflects a habit that has infuriated the Scots and the Welsh from time out of mind.

These glosses clearly belong to a time when Alsace was German-speaking. By the time of the war of 1870–1, Strasbourg had been part of France for almost 200 years, yet it still retained many signs of its German past. When annexed to France in 1681, it had been granted several privileges not enjoyed by other parts of the French kingdom, especially the right of unhampered Protestant worship. And German was still a usual everyday language in the city. The linguistic duality of Strasbourg, and of Alsace in general, is well reflected in the nineteenth-century scholars who worked on *The Garden of Delights*. Engelhardt, who lived in Strasbourg when it was a French city, wrote in German; Straub and Keller, who lived in Straßburg when it was a German city, wrote in French.

The uncertainty about where France ended and Germany began went back a thousand years. In the early Middle Ages there was no France, no Germany, just an enormous kingdom of the Franks, which by the year 800 extended from Barcelona to Hamburg and from the frontiers of Brittany to central Italy. It was the custom of the Franks to divide the kingdom between the sons of the ruler. When Louis, known as Louis the Pious, died in 840, his sons all wanted their share and fought for it. When two of them met at Strasbourg in 842 to swear oaths of alliance, the public declarations were made both in *Romana lingua*, that is, 'Romance', an early form of French, and *Teudisca lingua*, that is, 'Deutsch', German, so that followers from the western and the eastern parts of the Frankish realm could understand what was being said. After civil war and repeated subdivisions, a pattern emerged: north Italy went its own way, the western half of the empire (the kingdom of the West Franks) and the eastern half (the kingdom of the East Franks) faced each other over a contested middle ground ('the Middle Kingdom'). Eventually, in 925, after many decades, the Middle

Kingdom, named Lotharingia after one of its kings, was permanently attached to the kingdom of the East Franks. The kingdom of the West Franks is what we call France, the kingdom of the East Franks what we call Germany. Lotharingia was part of Germany but mainly French speaking (part of it is now Lorraine). In an age when language and nationality were not aligned or identified to a strong degree, this did not matter much.

Over the course of the following centuries, France and Germany developed very differently. In France the monarchy became stronger and the state more centralized, while in Germany political power came into the hands of local authorities – dukes, bishops, towns, and leagues like the Swiss Confederation. This was the background for the gradual expansion of France to the east, with the annexation of Strasbourg in 1681 a jewel in the crown of that process. The frontier between France and Germany was not a wild borderland. It was a line that went through some of the most populous and prosperous parts of western Europe and had come into existence purely as a result of the dynastic politics of the ninth century. It was fought over from the time it came into existence in the ninth century until the twentieth century. It is only since 1945 that the Franco-German frontier has attained what (we presume) to be permanent stability. Those centuries of Franco-German conflict explain why German shells fell on the once-German city of Strasbourg in 1870, annihilating *The Garden of Delights*, that treasure of medieval German art.

CHAPTER 7

Dublin, 30 June 1922: The Public Record Office of Ireland

To UNDERSTAND WHAT HAPPENED IN DUBLIN IN 1922, we need to start earlier. In October 1171 Henry II, king of England, landed in Ireland, near Waterford, the first king of England to set foot in the country. He certainly expected the Irish kings to recognize his overlordship, but this was more than a purely imperialist expedition. For several years previously, many of Henry's vassals and subjects, including great nobles and knights, had been fighting in Ireland, at first as the allies or mercenaries of Irish kings, but then on their own account. Amongst them were some whose loyalty Henry had reason to suspect. The king feared that the situation was getting out of control and responded by forbidding ships to sail from his dominions to Ireland and insisting that these free-lancers should return, fining them if they did not. The most important of these adventurers, Richard of Clare ('Strongbow' as he was nicknamed), crossed over to England and made his peace with the king. But Henry still thought his personal presence in Ireland desirable, hence the arrival of the royal fleet in October 1171. The king and his army stayed in Ireland for six months, throughout the winter, and Henry celebrated Christmas in Dublin in a palace specially built for the occasion, receiving the submission of Irish kings. The chronicler William of Newburgh expressed the epochal nature of these events: 'Ireland was never conquered or subordinated, never submitted to foreign rule, until the year 1171 from the Virgin Birth, which was the 18th year of Henry II, king of the English.'

From 1171 onwards the English Crown claimed and exercised authority in Ireland, sometimes more effectively, sometimes less so, with Dublin being the seat of royal administration from the time of Henry's Christmas feast until 1922. Starting with Henry's son, King John, the king of England also bore the title 'lord of Ireland', which was elevated to 'king of Ireland' in the time of Henry VIII, and then subsumed in the title 'king of the United Kingdom of Great Britain and Ireland' after the Act of Union of 1800. The royal administration in Ireland was supervised by the royal administration in England, and conscious efforts were undertaken to make the procedures and institutions uniform on both sides of the Irish Sea. In the 1220s the English government wrote to the justiciar of Ireland (the royal representative), making it clear that 'the laws of our land of Ireland and of England are and should be identical'. Ireland had counties, sheriffs, a Common Law like English Common Law, and (until 1800) a Parliament. All this administrative and legal machinery produced a large body of written material. From 1702, copies of official documents were archived in the newly created State Paper Office, located in Dublin Castle, although this obviously did not apply retrospectively, and in 1867 the Public Record Office of Ireland was founded, housed in the Four Courts complex, the home of Ireland's chief lawcourts, on the banks of the Liffey.

Over the course of the centuries, English rule never went uncontested. In the Middle Ages, the native royal dynasties survived, especially in the west and north where English settlement was less dense, and descendants of these dynasties, though now usually titled earls rather than kings, fought hard against Tudor efforts at a complete conquest. The Protestant Reformation reshaped this conflict, since most of the Irish population remained Catholic – in the sense of recognizing the supremacy of the pope and celebrating the Mass – while the English administration in Ireland and the English government were now Protestant (though many of the descendants of English settlers from earlier centuries were also Catholic). A political and military struggle that was national or racial now became also religious. In the seventeenth century, an effort was made to transform Ireland by the large-scale settlement of English and Scottish Protestant colonists, which had its deepest impact in the north, in Ulster. The abolition of a separate Irish Parliament in 1800 removed that local arena of political debate and discussion, and brought 100 Irish members into the UK Parliament, to make their points in Westminster, not hundreds of miles off in Dublin. Throughout the nineteenth century the so-called 'Irish Question' was debated in the British Parliament, sometimes with crucial political consequences. At the same time, Irish opposition to British rule was manifested in both non-violent and violent activism. The question of the restoration of a separate Irish Parliament ('Home Rule') polarized opinion, and the early twentieth century saw the formation of paramilitary organizations on both sides. The unsuccessful Easter Rising of 1916, when an attempt to declare an Irish republic in Dublin was suppressed by the British army, was followed, after the end of the Great War, by a sustained guerrilla campaign fought by Irish republicans against the forces of the British state, both army and police (many of whom were Irish). Republicans formed an army (the Irish Republican Army or IRA) and created a republican Parliament (the *Dáil*), which met clandestinely.

The year 1921 saw several crucial political developments. The British government established separate Parliaments in the north of Ireland, for the six counties with a large Protestant population, and in southern Ireland. The former was officially opened by the king, George V, in June and continued to meet until 1973, but the latter never had any real existence. Serious negotiations opened between the British government and republican representatives and resulted in the treaty of December 1921. This accepted the establishment of an Irish Free State with dominion status (like Canada), which gave practical autonomy but retained the king as head of state. It also allowed Northern Ireland to opt out of the Free State, thus endorsing the possibility of a division of Ireland, which is in fact what happened. The Irish representatives who signed the treaty had to take it back to Ireland for ratification by the republican *Dáil*. After fierce debate, the treaty was accepted by a vote of 64 to 57, one of the most vociferous opponents being Eamon de Valera, president of the republic (in the republican view). The two central issues at stake were the status of the future state – dominion of the British empire or republic – and partition of Ireland. Views were irreconcilable. Pro-treaty and anti-treaty parties moved from violent debate towards civil war.

After the treaty was ratified by the *Dáil* in January 1922, those who accepted it began the formation of the Provisional Government of the new Irish Free State, with

its own army (the 'National Army'), police, lawcourts, taxation and all the other instruments of a sovereign state, while
those opposed to the treaty rejected the authority of the
Provisional Government and began organizing opposition.
The IRA, which had fought the guerrilla war against the
British in 1919–21, split (although the name soon came to
designate only those opposed to the treaty and the government). Michael Collins was the leading figure of the
Provisional Government, Eamon de Valera the most celebrated of the political leaders of the republican opposition –
their rivalry went back years. In the background to all this was
the gradual withdrawal of British forces from southern
Ireland and the handover of key sites to the Provisional
Government: Dublin Castle was the one with the greatest
symbolic significance. Meanwhile, the (anti-treaty) IRA
began a campaign reminiscent of the guerrilla war of 1919–21
but now directed (mainly) at the Free State. They undertook
bank robberies to fund the acquisition of arms and took any
chance to seize strongpoints for the future struggle. On
13 April 1922, they occupied the Four Courts, that solidly
built complex in the centre of Dublin where the law courts
were accommodated, storing their munitions there and using
the Public Record Office of Ireland, housed in the complex, as
a place to prepare explosives: 'The inside was a jumble of
lathes, moulds and mine cases; hand-grenade bodies lay in
heaps; electric detonators, electric wires and explosives were
piled between the racks which held the records.'

The occupation of a central site in the capital by
armed men opposed to the Free State was a cause of concern
not only to the Provisional Government of the Free State but

also to the British government, which made plans for having the Four Courts stormed by British troops, who were still present in large numbers under the command of General Macready (a former military policeman, a specialist in dealing with civil unrest and a veteran of Egypt, India and South Africa, as well as the Great War). It was, according to his own account in *Annals of an Active Life*, Macready's opposition to the proposal, 'which I thought flavoured strongly of Mr. Winston Churchill's feverish impetuosity', and his subsequent delay in implementing it, that led the British government to reconsider its plan for a British attack on the Four Courts. Soon after this, Rory O'Connor, one of the fierier of the IRA men in the Four Courts, authorized the kidnapping of an important general of the National Army, 'Ginger' O'Connell, a step that convinced Michael Collins that he would have to deal with the situation through force. He borrowed two 18-pounder field guns from General Macready (a transaction authorized by the British government), and on 28 June 1922 the shelling began – a date that is taken to mark the beginning of the Irish Civil War.

The shelling lasted three days. More ammunition and more artillery had to be sought from the British army. During that time, parts of the Four Courts caught fire, and the flames eventually spread to the munitions. Around midday on 30 June an enormous explosion shook Dublin, and the Public Records of Ireland went up in flames. Charred fragments of its documents were found some 12 miles (20 kilometres) away. The IRA garrison surrendered later that day. The fire eventually burned itself out. The Civil War continued. On 22 August Michael Collins was killed in an IRA ambush, but the Free

Figure 11. The destruction of the Public Record Office of Ireland on
30 June 1922. Culture Club / Hulton Archive / Getty Images.

State eventually prevailed. Eamon de Valera spent some time in
prison but in 1932, in a remarkable turn of fortune, became
head of the Irish government. Ireland's status as a republic was
established in two steps, in 1937 and 1949. But the path there
had seen, in that explosion in 1922, the destruction of a vast part
of the record of Ireland's past.

Such an event was bound to generate angrily
conflicting views. The Irish Civil War, despite fatalities
that are very low by twentieth-century standards, left an

inheritance of deep antagonisms, which continued to shape Irish history. The two main parties in the Free State, and subsequently the Republic, Fine Gael and de Valera's Fianna Fáil, descended directly from earlier pro- and anti-treaty groups, while Sinn Féin (in various forms) and the IRA continued what they described as the 'war of national liberation', aimed at reuniting Ireland under a republic. Perhaps because the issues of the Irish Civil War are still sharp, modern Irish historians often describe the cause of the destruction of the Public Record Office of Ireland in 1922, somewhat coyly, as 'the fire'. At the time, opinions were more forthright and always had political implications. For example, while it was universally acknowledged that the Free State had asked for and received its artillery from the British army, the IRA also insisted that British officers had participated in the firing of the artillery, something that would underline the Free State's betrayal of the national cause. On the other side, General Macready wrote of 'The senseless destruction of the Four Courts by the Republicans after they had made up their minds to surrender.' The National Government, like the British, claimed that the IRA had blown up the buildings.

There is some evidence that members of the garrison had determined to set fire to the buildings rather than evacuate them. Ernie O'Malley, one of the leaders of the anti-treaty fighters inside the complex, reports two exchanges with Paddy O'Brien, the commander of the garrison. One took place before the assault, when negotiations were taking place:

> I had a talk with Paddy O'Brien . . . 'We don't all approve of
> the negotiations', I said, 'they are to kill time.' 'That's just
> it,' said O'Brien. 'I know what I'm going to do. I'll blow up
> or burn the Four Courts rather than hand them over.' 'I'm
> with you in that case,' I said. Next day barrels of petrol and
> paraffin were stored in the cellars and dark corners,
> unknown to the rest of the Headquarters Staff.

The second conversation was later, during the fighting, when
the 'Munitions' building was threatened:

> Paddy O'Brien met me after the staff meeting. 'Munitions
> is a weak post, Paddy,' I said . . . 'I know,' he said. 'The only
> thing left for me is to burn it out, and I think I'll do that . . . '
> He had decided to burn out munitions as he felt it could no
> longer be held. The block contained the Irish archives and
> it had suffered more than any other of our buildings from
> shellfire.

O'Malley reports that O'Brien sent a lieutenant to destroy the
building, but it was too late, since the National Army troops
had already seized it. It appears that the combination of raging
fires and substantial amounts of explosives and flammable
material was in itself sufficient to generate the enormous
explosion.

Mutual blaming naturally follows such events. After
the Germans destroyed Louvain University Library in 1940
(having done the same in 1914), they said it was the British
who had set fire to it: 'A German investigation committee . . .
which had discovered tins in the basement originating from
the Far East, alleged that they had been packed with gasoline
by the British who then set them off with three grenades.' The

level of destruction that occurred in Dublin in 1922 was in fact the result of a combination of actions by the two sides: the IRA storing and manufacturing munitions in the Four Courts buildings and the Free State forces shelling it. The danger of having records and explosives in close proximity had been pointed out long before by the Parliamentary committee into the Ashburnham House fire of 1731 (discussed in Chapter 4). They noted that the records stored in the White Tower of the Tower of London were 'in good condition . . . but underneath are stores of gunpowder belonging to the Office of Ordnance' – exactly the situation in 1922.

The records that were destroyed in 1922 did not constitute the whole story of Ireland but were mainly the record of colonial Ireland. England has one of the richest archives of medieval documents in the world, and 'English Ireland', that is, the parts of the island effectively controlled by the English administration, followed the example of the English government in producing parchment rolls that recorded the work of the various parts of the Irish administration: chancery, Exchequer, the lawcourts and Parliament. From the thirteenth to the nineteenth centuries, most official government records were stored in Dublin Castle, though not always in good conditions, while frequently officials kept records at home, and there were occasional dramatic losses of material, as in the fire at St Mary's abbey in 1304, when a large number of chancery rolls being stored there were destroyed. After the Public Record Office of Ireland was founded in 1867, an energetic policy of centralization was followed, with the attempt to bring as many records as possible into the care of the new institution. Almost all of this was incinerated in 1922: 485 of the 488 medieval plea rolls, which recorded the activities of the royal lawcourts, all the statute rolls of the Irish Parliament, etc. Losses also included more recent records of genealogical value, such as parish registers, wills and census returns of the seventeenth, eighteenth and nineteenth centuries, and anyone researching Irish ancestry is made aware immediately of how much more difficult this is than researching English ancestry because of these huge gaps in Irish genealogical records.

It is possible to have a fairly good idea of what was lost because, three years before the Civil War, Herbert Wood, Deputy Keeper of the Public Records, had published *A Guide to the Records deposited in the Public Record Office of Ireland*, which, in 300 or so pages, preserves the memory of the rich archive that was destroyed – fifty-five pages listing the various classes of document from the chancery, sixty-three pages those from the Exchequer, along with a great miscellany of material ('Huguenot Records', 'Irish Railway Commission'). Wood (1860–1955) was born in Lambeth, south London, of an Irish father and an English mother, graduated from Oxford with a degree in divinity and classics, and in 1884 took up a job with the Public Record Office of Ireland, where he remained for the rest of his working life. Given what happened three years after publication of his *Guide*, there is a poignancy in its opening words:

> The Public Records of Ireland, like those of most countries, have undergone great vicissitudes, but have perhaps suffered more in the way of loss of valuable material for history. When the history of Ireland in the past is taken

into account, it is more to be wondered at that so much has survived from the chaotic conditions which prevailed in this country.

Even sadder is another comment of his: 'The centralisation of the Public Records in one building has been attended with excellent results.'

The catastrophe of 1922 illustrates the danger in having a central record repository, since it means a large amount of material is vulnerable in one place. Irish medieval records that had *not* been deposited in the Public Record Office of Ireland had a far greater chance of survival than those that were. As Herbert Wood later noted, perhaps thinking wryly of his earlier views, 'the method of assembling the public records under one roof was the very means of making such a destruction possible'. One reaction to the loss was an undertaking to get Ireland's manuscript sources into print, in the form of the creation of the Irish Manuscripts Commission in 1928, a body dedicated to publishing Irish historical material of all periods, which clocked up an impressive number of 158 volumes in its first 80 years, in addition to the texts published in its journal, *Analecta Hibernica*.

After the disaster, efforts were soon made to see what could be saved from the records of Ireland's medieval (and early modern) past. The hunt focused on several broad categories of material. The first was surviving original documents from the Public Record Office. Some of these had survived because they were in the Reading Room, not in the section of the building where records were stored, and the Reading Room had been less damaged by the fire. Others were seriously damaged but not completely destroyed. A list of medieval and other records that had been salvaged was published in 1928.

A far more important source than the sad fragments from the Record Office was provided by the records that had been summarized, copied or published before 1922. The study and transcription of medieval Irish records began long before the creation of the modern Record Office. In the seventeenth century, for example, the antiquarian James Ware (d. 1666), a graduate of Trinity College Dublin and an active royalist, devoted time to copying, or ordering the copying, of a vast mass of miscellaneous material, in Latin, English and Irish, relating to Irish history. The catalogue of his collection which he had printed in 1648 lists ninety-three manuscripts, which included both medieval manuscripts and volumes of his own transcripts and copies, and he continued collecting and copying after that. On his death, his books were purchased by the earl of Clarendon, brother-in-law of James II, and many of them eventually found their way to the Bodleian Library in Oxford, among the Rawlinson manuscripts, or the British Library, among the Additional Manuscripts, where they can still be consulted.

An example is British Library, Additional Manuscript 4787, a volume of 322 folios containing an astonishing miscellany of material, which includes notes from the Red Book of the Irish Exchequer, which was destroyed in 1922; extracts from many chronicles, such as the so-called 'Kilkenny Chronicle' and the Annals of Inisfallen (the original manuscript of which was also in Ware's possession); many charters, among them a grant by Henry II in 1177 of the kingdom of Desmond to two of the first Norman conquerors in Ireland, Robert fitz Stephen and Miles de Cogan, and a charter of William Marshal (the Younger), earl of Pembroke, founding the hospital of St John the Evangelist at Kilkenny (a document that survives nowhere else); accounts of the Irish bishoprics in the king's hands through vacancy in 1282; a catalogue of Irish saints; and so on. British Library, Additional Manuscript 4790, another manuscript from Ware's collection, consists of copies of entries in the medieval plea rolls and Pipe Rolls (the records of the annual audit of royal revenue) stored in the Bermingham Tower, Dublin Castle, made by Thomas Chetham, Keeper of the Records (d. 1624). Ware owned at least eight medieval cartularies containing the documents of Irish monasteries, and almost all of these were eventually transmitted to the Bodleian Library or other public collections, while the transcripts he made from cartularies that he did not own are, in many cases, the only surviving evidence of the documents, as the volumes themselves are no longer traceable.

Sir James Ware is a perfect model of the energetic upper-class individual, devoted to antiquarian and historical research, whose work helped save the medieval past by preserving its manuscript records. Once the state began to recognize that it had a public duty to do the same, different funding and different procedures produced the tax-based bureaucratic bodies that have taken up this task over the last few centuries. The first British Record Commission was established in 1800 'to inquire into the state of the Public Records', and subsequent Commissions worked until 1837, publishing reports and dozens of volumes of original source material, including the earliest Pipe Roll; the earliest chancery rolls, from the reigns of John and Henry III; the *Statutes of the Realm* (to the reign of Queen Anne); *The Acts of Parliament of Scotland* and much else. The Irish Record Commission was established in 1810, ten years after the British, with a remit to 'methodize, regulate and digest' the Irish state records and produce printed summaries and indexes of them, and it continued work until 1830. In that time, it faced obstruction on the part of jealous officials, accusations of 'inefficiency and extravagance' and exhibited 'an extreme lack of organization', but, nonetheless, it did produce in print, apart from annual reports (which themselves included historical documents), half-a-dozen volumes of calendars of record material from the twelfth to the seventeenth centuries (calendars are chronological lists with a summary of each item), and, surviving in manuscript, more then 200 volumes of calendars and indexes.

Margaret Griffith (1911–2001), who worked in the Public Record Office of Ireland from 1944 and headed it from 1956 to 1971, concluded, in a paper she wrote about the Irish Record Commission in 1950:

> The history of the Irish record commission is thus in the main one of frustration and wasted effort, and its productions, if it were not for the circumstances which unhappily make them in most cases our only substitutes for destroyed originals, would be of no very considerable value. In the existing circumstances, however, they form one of our most important collections of historical material, and whatever their defects, and whatever the waste and inefficiency involved in their compilation, their mere existence has now become a matter for thankfulness to the historian.

So, 'better than nothing' is the conclusion.

For the Irish Record Commission of 1810–30 'making a copy' of a manuscript meant transcribing it longhand. Within a decade, however, a revolutionary new way of making copies was being invented and refined: photography. This technique could be applied to producing facsimiles of medieval manuscripts and thus ensuring the survival of the image, if not the object. In the years 1874–84, J. T. Gilbert of the recently formed Public Record Office of Ireland oversaw the publication of the five volumes of *Facsimiles of National Manuscripts of Ireland*, which contained more than 260 images of books and documents from or relevant to medieval Ireland. These included not only the great treasures of medieval Irish culture such as the Book of Kells or the Book of Leinster but also the more pragmatic documents of the English administration, including extracts from the chancery rolls, the statute rolls of the Irish Parliament and the Red Book of the Irish Exchequer, which were all housed in the Irish Public Record Office and hence incinerated in 1922.

Facsimiles, copies and transcripts from the period before 1922 could thus be used to reconstruct some of the material destroyed in 1922. An example of the meticulous and time-consuming work that was devoted to this task of reconstruction is an article from 1966 by the distinguished historian from Trinity College Dublin, James Lydon. He focused on the memoranda rolls of the Irish Exchequer in the period 1294–1509. These recorded many diverse transactions, such as payments by the sheriffs, writs received from England or from the Irish chancery, lawsuits heard in the Exchequer, records of debts, outgoing writs and summonses, etc. He began by pointing out the scale of the loss: 'Of the memoranda rolls compiled at the Irish Exchequer during the period . . . only 147 (out of approximately 220) survived in the Public Record Office of Ireland in 1922. To-day there are two.' So, two-thirds of them had survived from the Tudor period to 1922, but only 1.5 per cent of those made it through 1922. Recovery work could begin with the calendar prepared by the Irish Record Commission. This consists of forty-three large manu-script volumes, which, along with the two surviving original rolls, constitute our main source of knowledge of this mater-ial. Lydon recognized the inadequacies of this calendar, its omissions and errors, but, of course, sometimes the alterna-tive was nothing. In addition, he listed transcripts from other sources, almost entirely kept in Irish repositories, although he included a few items from Sir James Ware's manuscripts in the British Library. Lydon provided a list (fifty-seven pages long) of all the memoranda rolls that survived in 1922 and where extracts from them could now be found.

Another crucial source for medieval Irish records is England. In the Middle Ages many Irish records came to England, either as duplicates of those in Ireland or as originals sent to England for some reason – for example, in the later Middle Ages records of the Irish Exchequer were sent to England for audit. Most such documents, if they survived, would end up eventually in the Public Record Office in London, which is now subsumed in the National Archives in Kew. Awareness of the importance of English records for Irish history was nothing new in 1922 – in 1875–86 the Irish lawyer and scholar H. S. Sweetman had published a *Calendar of Documents relating to Ireland preserved in Her Majesty's*

Public Record Office, London, 1171–1307, which contains 8,351 entries – but the destruction of the Irish Public Record Office made the hunt for such material, especially for documents that had been sent over from Ireland in the Middle Ages, of far greater significance.

Philomena Connolly (1948–2002), who was from 1971 an archivist at the Public Record Office of Ireland (later renamed the National Archives of Ireland), took up the torch from Sweetman, calendaring Irish Exchequer material from the British Public Record Office in *Irish Exchequer Payments, 1270–1446* (the early entries actually overlap with Sweetman's). She went on to edit the statute rolls of the late medieval Irish Parliament (these based on modern transcripts), as well as providing a clear and incisive guide to the relevant archive materials in *Medieval Record Sources*, both works published in 2002. In 2005, a survey of the medieval Irish material in the National Archives at Kew was published by Paul Dryburgh and Brendan Smith. It runs to well over 300 pages, and, in the introduction, the authors explain how such a mass of material came to find its home in London. Pursuing this same direction, a project entitled 'CIRCLE: A Calendar of Irish Chancery Letters c. 1244 – 1509' was initiated in 2012 under the direction of Peter Crooks of Trinity College Dublin, and this eventually published online a calendar of 20,000 letters.

Beginning in 2016, Ireland went through a frenzy of centenaries, most of them not free from elements of controversy: the Easter Rising of 1916, Partition, the Anglo-Irish Treaty of 1921. Inspired by the approaching centenary in 2022 of the Civil War and the destruction of the Public

Record Office, a major international project ('Beyond 2022') was organized, with the participation of the National Archives (Ireland), the National Archives (UK), the Public Record Office of Northern Ireland (Belfast), the Irish Manuscripts Commission and the Library, Trinity College Dublin, as well as many other institutions, to recreate what was lost, as far as possible. In its own words, it was 'an all-island and international collaborative research project working to create a virtual reconstruction of the Public Record Office of Ireland'. Like the Chancery Letters project, it was headed by Peter Crooks of Trinity, and it issued periodic reports online in 'Archive Fever' (a sly nod to Jacques Derrida's *Archive Fever: A Freudian Impression*, published in English in 1996). The project created a three-dimensional computer model of the Public Record Office of Ireland as it was before 1922. Each of the shelving bays of this virtual archive leads to the documents that represent what was shelved in that bay, be they medieval documents preserved elsewhere or modern transcripts. It is conceived as an ongoing project. The bulk of Ireland's medieval records were destroyed in an afternoon; the work of reconstruction is now in its second century. Destruction is easier than reconstruction.

As mentioned, the destruction of 1922 mainly affected the records of the colonial administration of Ireland. There are other manuscripts from medieval Ireland that have come down to the present day and shed light on Irish society of the past. First, there are the materials that survive from those parts of Ireland that were not subjugated or settled, or only weakly so, where native Irish (Gaelic) continued as the dominant language. Apart from

Figure 12. The virtual reconstruction of the Public Record Office of Ireland, 2022. Virtual Record Treasury of Ireland.

the famous manuscripts of the early Middle Ages, Irish culture survived and thrived during later centuries: bardic poetry, epics and annals in Irish are to be found in four- teenth- and fifteenth-century compilations, like the Yellow Book of Lecan, written around 1400 in the far west of Ireland, and in manuscripts of the early modern period, which are often copies of medieval manuscripts no longer extant. Bardic poetry has been explored with particularly illuminat- ing results by Katharine Simms of Trinity College Dublin. Second, there are records from the areas that were settled by men and women of Norman, English and Welsh descent, so 'colonial' in a sense, but they were not produced by the royal administration. Aristocratic families, religious institutions and towns all had archives, and these often survive, as long as they had not been transferred to the Public Record Office of Ireland before 1922.

An example of this colonial but non-royal documentation is provided by a volume of around seventy folios produced in 1408 which contains charters and other documents relating to the property of the Welsh monastery of Llanthony Prima in Ireland (there were two monasteries with this name, distinguished as *Prima* – 'First' – and *Secunda* – 'Second'). Llanthony Prima had been founded by a member of the Lacy family, which was very generously endowed with land in Ireland after Henry II's arrival in 1171, and the Lacys had continued their patronage by grants to Llanthony of lands and revenues in Meath and elsewhere. The volume from 1408 is a 'Register of the lands of the house of Llanthony Prima in Ireland' made by two canons who had been appointed as legal representatives of the priory. The opening pages record grants from John Cumin, archbishop of Dublin (1181–1212), the first Englishman to hold this position, so they go back to the early days of the colony. Subsequent documents date to the thirteenth and fourteenth centuries, culminating in a seven-folio survey and valuation of all the Llanthony possessions in Ireland as of 1408.

The transmission of the Register was complex. In 1481, Llanthony Prima was made a dependency of Llanthony Secunda, outside Gloucester, and the Register was apparently transferred to that house. When Henry VIII and his minister Thomas Cromwell determined on the suppression of the monasteries and the seizure of their property, Llanthony Secunda and its lands were granted to Arthur Porter, 'the king's servant', a member of a local gentry family, in 1540 or early 1541. In this way, the Register, and other volumes containing the property records of the priory, came into the hands of the Porter family, and later passed by marriage into the possession of the Scudamores, a notable Herefordshire family, who bore the title Viscount Scudamore from 1628 to 1716, when the last viscount died, leaving an only daughter, Frances, as his heir. Frances married Henry Somerset, duke of Beaufort, who took the name Scudamore, but the marriage ended in an acrimonious and scandalous divorce (at one point the duke had to take a virility test to refute Frances' claim that he was impotent). Frances remarried to Charles Fitzroy, who took the name Fitzroy-Scudamore, but she died soon after giving birth to a daughter. This daughter, heir to the family fortune, married the heir to the dukedom of Norfolk but became mentally unstable and was certified as 'lunatic'. 'Lunatics' were the responsibility of the chancery and came under the supervision of Masters in Chancery.

The website of the National Archive in Kew explains what happened next to the Llanthony documents:

> The exhibits in this series entered the office of John Springett Harvey, Master in Chancery, after the lord chancellor had, on 7 August 1816, instructed Thomas Braithwaite, steward of the duchess of Norfolk, to commission Thomas Bird, a Hereford solicitor, to compile an inventory of them. Frances Scudamore, widow of Charles Howard, 11th duke of Norfolk, being childless and deemed lunatic, was provided for until her death on 22 October 1820. Her archive entered Chancery as exhibits in connection with her maintenance.

From chancery, the Register passed to the Public Record Office, where it was given the reference C/115/80 – 'C' for 'chancery' and 115 indicating the records of Harvey, Master in Chancery, and the duchess of Norfolk's deeds – and was later incorporated into the National Archives at Kew. More than 600 years after its creation, and having survived the destruction of the monasteries, and scandal and madness among the aristocracy, it can be studied for historical purposes. Hence it is now possible to take a London underground train to Kew and read a detailed picture of the rural world of Meath in 1408: names of tenants, levels of rent, labour services owed, death duties, field names, crops sown and so forth. From such concrete details, a true picture of the past may be drawn up.

CHAPTER 8

Naples, 30 September 1943: The State Archive

M ODERN ITALY WAS CREATED AS A SOVEREIGN state, covering the peninsula and the islands of Sicily and Sardinia, in several steps. The most important was in 1860, when almost every Italian region accepted the sovereignty of the king of Sardinia, who, in addition to the island of Sardinia, ruled north-west Italy (Piedmont). In the next decade, the remaining areas of Italy (Venice, Rome) followed suit. The previous time Italy had been politically united was more than thirteen centuries earlier, under the Ostrogothic king Theodoric the Great (493–526) and his immediate successors. However, from 535 to 1860 Italy was a fragmented land. During those years, the political pattern changed constantly: in the sixth century, the peninsula was divided between the Byzantine empire and Lombard kings and dukes; in the eighth century, the Lombard kingdom was conquered by the Franks and became part of the Carolingian empire; in the ninth century, the Muslims conquered Sicily and established a foothold on the mainland; in the eleventh century, Norman adventurers turned up and, over the course of decades, took over the Lombard duchies, the Byzantine parts of southern Italy and Muslim Sicily, and, in 1130, crowned this enterprise by consolidating their conquests into a new kingdom – the kingdom of Sicily, as it was known, although it included not only the island of Sicily but also most of southern Italy. Especially in its early centuries, it was a place marked by the coexistence of different faiths – Latin Christian, Greek Christian, Jewish and Muslim – and languages – Romance, Latin, Greek, Hebrew and Arabic. This kingdom (the *Regno* as Italian historians often label it) survived until 1860.

The kingdom of Sicily was one of the most powerful players in the politics of medieval Europe. It was wealthy, relatively centralized, and ruled by a series of determined and aggressive kings and queens: the Norman dynasty 1130–94, the Hohenstaufen dynasty 1194–1266, the Angevin dynasty 1266–1435. In 1282, the island of Sicily rebelled against the Angevin kings and called in the Aragonese to secure their independence, and for the rest of the Middle Ages, with one short exception (1442–58), there were thus two kingdoms, one on the mainland, one on the island. The mainland kingdom was often referred to as the kingdom of Naples, from its chief city, although the official title of both realms remained the kingdom of Sicily – hence, when they were finally reunited, the title 'kingdom of the Two Sicilies'.

Italy was one of the more literate parts of medieval Europe, and the government of the kingdom of Sicily generated a huge body of official records. In the Angevin period, a series of registers was kept. The nineteenth-century archivist who had seen these volumes long before their destruction described their contents: 'laws and statutes for the administration of the kingdom, privileges and grants for individuals and communities, grants of fiefs, mandates and letters to officials, letters to other parts of Italy, Provence, Anjou, France and elsewhere, sentences of the Great Court, proclamations of peace, of war, of alliance, investiture of canons and prebendaries'. Obviously, such material would be a rich source for historians writing the history of the kingdom of Sicily/Naples.

Like the rest of Europe, the kingdom of Naples experienced radical changes during the period of the French Revolution. The Parthenopean Republic of 1799 and the violent restoration of the monarchy under King Ferdinand have been mentioned in Chapter 2, but in December 1805 Napoleon decreed the deposition of Ferdinand, who again fled to the island of Sicily. This time, however, the monarchy was not to be replaced by a republic. Although the French Revolution had abolished the French monarchy and cut off the head of the king, once Napoleon seized state power, he soon came to think that an imperial title would suit him well and, in 1804, crowned himself 'Emperor of the French' in Notre-Dame in Paris. The novelist Stendhal has a telling anecdote about this, describing Napoleon returning from the ceremony, chatting to the distinguished soldier, Antoine-Guillaume Delmas:

> 'What a fine ceremony, Delmas; really superb!' said the Emperor, on his return from Notre-Dame.
>
> 'Yes, General, the only thing missing was the two million men killed in trying to overthrow what you're just setting up!'
>
> Next day Delmas was exiled, with orders not to come within forty leagues of Paris.

Having acquired a taste for a crown, Napoleon decided to share its pleasures with his relatives, and from 1804 to 1814 his brothers were elevated to fine titles. His older brother, Joseph Bonaparte, became king of Naples in place of Ferdinand, though his authority never extended to the island of Sicily. In 1808, Joseph was promoted to be king of Spain, and Napoleon's brother-in-law, the dashing general Joachim Murat, became king of Naples in succession to Joseph, though, as a condition, he had to adopt the surname 'Napoleon' (some might see this as evidence of Bonaparte's megalomania). It was during Murat's reign that the state archive of Naples (the General Archive of the Kingdom) was founded, in December 1808, by 'an ordinance to reorganize and unite in one place the ancient archives of the kingdom'. This was no secret tool of the state – 'the use of all the archives is public', the law declared. One huge body of records that went into the state archives at this time was the accumulated documents of the monasteries of the kingdom, almost all of which had been suppressed in 1806–8, under Joseph Bonaparte and Murat. Later in the century, Giuseppe Del Giudice, the archivist of the state archive, described the 347 volumes of monastic 'parchments' lining the shelves in the archive, along with 200 loose seals that had fallen from these documents.

Giuseppe Del Giudice (1819–1909) was an archivist in the heroic mould. In the preface to the first volume of his edition of the documents of Charles I of Sicily he wrote:

> Hard and arduous work is that which I undertake to
> publish, but neither the difficulty of the task nor the
> considerable obstacles which stood before me have been

able to discourage my spirit and keep me back from putting
into effect an idea yearned for from my earliest youth.

This idea was to publish the documents that illustrated 'the
true history' of the ancient government of southern Italy.
'And these documents existed', he continued, 'in the
General Archive of Naples, for the most part forgotten or
disregarded.' The first volume of Del Giudice's collection of
documents was published in 1863, just after the first big step to
Italian unification, and he had strong opinions about this,
which he expressed in the preface to the volume. In the
thirteenth century, he wrote, Italy had been divided between
two political groupings, the Guelphs and the Ghibellines. Del
Giudice judged that the former, who represented the semi-
independent cities of northern Italy and the papacy, supported liberty but did not consider national unity, while the
latter, partisans of the emperor and the Hohenstaufen,
renounced civil liberty but had a strong sense of national
unity. It was only, wrote Del Giudice, when liberty and
nationalism were reconciled that Italy could rise again, as
she had just done.

Whatever one thinks of this analysis, it is clear that
Del Giudice thought archives had a part to play in presenting
the national story. He tells an anecdote, perhaps imaginary, of
an official in revolutionary France: 'In 1793 a Minister of the
Interior in France said, when speaking of the ancient documents in the archives, that it would be better to replace 'these
old and ridiculous pieces of waste paper with the simple
Declaration of the Rights of Man'. But there were two faces
to the French Revolution: the revolution of the Terror and the

revolution of the Enlightenment – one sought to destroy the past (as in the case of the documents burnt in the Place Vendôme in 1792, mentioned in Chapter 1, and the proclamation of that year as Year One), the other to create a rational, bureaucratic, centralized state. This is not to mention the Napoleonic dream of a French continental empire, which was in a long tradition of French expansionism but had never before met such success, as French armies occupied Madrid in 1808 and Moscow in 1813. This series of conquests is what brought Joseph Bonaparte and Joachim 'Napoleon' to the throne of Naples and with them a host of modernizing measures that came at the same time as the new state archive – the Napoleonic Code, a meritocratic civil service, reform of the military academy and university, foundation of an observatory, botanical gardens, and (in the same month as the archive) a National Bank. King Ferdinand returned to Naples, for the third time, after the fall of Napoleon in 1815, but maintained a few of the innovations of the Napoleonic period, including the state archive, which, in 1845, was given a handsome new home in the former Benedictine monastery of St Severinus and St Sossius, where it is still located.

The Neapolitan archives suffered losses over the course of time, sometimes by deliberate destruction, as in 1701, as we have seen in Chapter 5, but these earlier incidents were all to be overshadowed by the catastrophic event of 30 September 1943. To explain this, it is necessary to go back to the rise of fascism in Italy. The term 'fascist' has a precise origin, even if it is no longer precisely applied. The Italian word *fascio* means 'bundle' or 'bunch', and, from the late nineteenth century, it was applied to popular or workers' organizations, and later to nationalist groups. Members of such groups were thus *fascisti*. In 1921, the National Fascist Party was established under the leadership of Benito Mussolini, and it attained state power the following year. The label 'fascist' was soon applied to other nationalist movements in other countries and eventually became such a general term of abuse that it lost its meaning, but from 1922 to 1943 there was a Fascist Party, so-named, that ran Italy. Mussolini, at first the senior partner of Hitler, since he had pioneered the role of an ultra-nationalist authoritarian 'great leader', found himself outpaced by the slightly younger but more ruthless man (there were six years between them). On 1 September 1939, Hitler invaded Poland; on 2 September, Italy declared its neutrality; on 3 September, Britain and France declared war on Germany. Thus, it looked as if Mussolini had decided to sit this one out. However, after the Germans occupied Denmark, Norway, the Netherlands and Belgium in the spring of 1940, Italy now declared war on Britain and France. For some years Germany and Italy worked together as allies, in North Africa and elsewhere. But once allied forces landed in Sicily in July 1943, Italian opponents of Mussolini's regime, acting together with the king, were emboldened enough to force the dictator to resign, to imprison him, to abolish the Fascist Party, and to begin negotiations for an armistice with the British and American forces. This was signed on 3 September and Italy's unconditional surrender announced on 8 September.

The German forces stationed in Italy were not going to tolerate this. Overnight they went from being an army of allies to an army of occupation. On 12 September 1943, they freed Mussolini from captivity, and a few days later he declared the formation of a Republican Fascist Party, allied with Germany. German troops disarmed most of the Italian army, despite sporadic resistance, and occupied the chief cities of Italy. Allied prisoners of war in Italian custody were transported across the Alps to Germany. Meanwhile allied troops landed on the mainland and moved north towards Naples. A period of chaos followed in the city. The top Italian generals in Naples abandoned the city to the Germans, but there was local resistance of a disorganized nature, especially when the Germans imposed a policy of deporting the inhabitants for forced labour. German soldiers and Neapolitans were killed, and the fighting culminated in the so-called Four Days of Naples, 27–30 September, with armed insurgents and German soldiers engaged in constant hostilities. The German army had already decided to withdraw from Naples. Hitler had ordered them to leave nothing behind but mud and ashes, although the resistance that the Germans encountered in the city and the speed of the allied advance meant that acts of destruction could only be local and opportunistic. One such act of vandalism was directed against the Naples State Archives.

The head of the Naples State Archives at this time was Count Riccardo Filangieri (1882–1959), a member of an ancient Neapolitan noble family, whose namesake had played an important part in the warfare and politics of Italy and the Crusader states in the thirteenth century. He wrote an account of the events of 30 September 1943 which was later translated into English and published in *The American Archivist* of October 1944. In it he describes how, to escape the bombing of Naples by the Allies, which had been going on intensively since December 1942, he had arranged 'the transfer of the most valuable historical documents of the State Archives of Naples to the Montesano villa near San Paolo Belsito, about thirty kilometers [20 miles] from Naples. In the halls of that solid building there [were] thus deposited more than 30,000 volumes and about 50,000 parchments.' In September 1943, after Italy's surrender to the Allies, the region had become full of squads of German soldiers, armed with submachine guns, who took livestock, seized men for forced labour, plundered houses and burned key installations, such as mills, warehouses and railway stations.

Filangieri continues:

> When the Allied Army was already near, in the afternoon of September 28, there appeared at Montesano villa a squad of three German soldiers in search of calves. When the soldiers did not find the calves which they knew existed, they entered with violence the ground floor of the villa, where they saw the great pile of cases containing the documents. When asked what those cases contained, the archives personnel living in the villa informed them of the presence in that depository of the historical documents of the State Archives of Naples. Having learned this, they went away without saying anything. The next morning, September 29, there appeared at the Montesano villa an officer and another soldier, who wished to visit the rooms where the documents were. He had one of the cases opened and they examined the volumes. The director [Antonio Capograssi] informed them of the importance of these documents, furnishing them all suitable explanations to

demonstrate the purely cultural character of that
depository. After having examined everything, the officer
said: 'All right,' and left.

Filangieri, who was living in a villa nearby, received reports of
what had happened and decided to write a letter addressed to
the local German commander, describing what the depository
contained and explaining that the documents were of only
historical interest. This he sent to the Montesano villa on
30 September.

> One of the archives guards who took my letter to the
> Montesano villa at about 9:15 met a squad of three German
> soldiers on motorcycles armed, as usual, with submachine
> guns, who were going towards the villa. They had hardly
> arrived when they announced that within fifteen minutes
> they would set fire to the whole depository of documents.
> Then my letter was handed to the man who was
> commanding the squad. And as this man did not
> understand Italian the letter was entirely translated for
> him. After the German had listened to the letter he brutally
> snatched the letter and the lists of documents and,
> throwing them into the air, shouted: 'Commander know
> everything, order burn.' The director vainly sought to
> obtain a delay in order to warn me and to send my letter to
> the commander; the three soldiers immediately began the
> work of destruction by placing paper, straw, and
> gunpowder in the four corners and in the center of each
> room and by setting the fire in such a way that in a few
> minutes the whole villa became an immense pyre. After
> assuring themselves that the fire could not be extinguished,

they went away but returned an hour later to make certain
that the work of destruction was complete.

Hundreds of volumes and thousands of documents had gone
up in flames. As Filangieri wrote in *The American Archivist*,
'their destruction has created an immense void in the historical sources of European civilization, a void which nothing
will ever be able to fill'.

Filangieri regarded the destruction of the 378 volumes
of the registers of the Angevin chancery covering the activities
of the Angevin dynasty from 1266 to 1435 as one of the most
serious losses and resolved to initiate what turned out to be
a heroic undertaking to rescue what could be saved from the
disaster. His method was similar to that employed in Ireland
in the wake of the destruction of the Irish Public Record
Office – the hunt for antiquarian transcripts, duplicates, documents in recipient archives and so forth. He calculated that at
least 350 scholars had worked on the registers in the decades
before the war and circulated them with requests for their
notes, microfilms and photographs of documents. An early
respondent was the British medievalist Evelyn Mary Jamison
(1877–1972). She had studied at one of the first women's
colleges at Oxford, Lady Margaret Hall, from 1898 to 1901, at
a time when women were not allowed to be awarded degrees,
but had gone on to be an expert in the history of Norman
Sicily. She was familiar with the archives at Naples and, in an
article of 1949 titled 'Documents from the Angevin Registers
of Naples: Charles I', answered Filangieri's call by publishing
'the present small collection of 303 items', being transcripts of
entries in the register of Charles I of Sicily (1265/6–85),

made either by Evelyn Jamison herself or by, or for, two other British scholars who had worked on the material. Meanwhile, Filangieri had organized a department of the archives dedicated to 'reconstructing' the Angevin registers. Backed by the world-famous philosopher and historian Benedetto Croce, the project also got the Accademia Pontaniana, Naples' most ancient learned society, to support the publication of the reconstructed registers. Between 1950 and 2010 fifty volumes were published, under the successive leadership of Filangieri, Jole Mazzoleni (1908–91) and Stefano Palmieri, that covered the period 1265–95.

Two brief examples will show the type of material that the Registers contained and which would have been lost without the work of archivists and other scholars before 1943. One concerns the very earliest documents from the Angevin Registers. In 1265, the kingdom of Sicily was ruled by Manfred, son of Frederick II, of the Hohenstaufen dynasty, but the pope was desperate to remove him and install a prince from a friendlier dynasty. He had eventually settled on Charles of Anjou (hence the adjective Angevin), brother of Louis IX of France, and on 28 June 1265 he invested him with the kingdom of Sicily. Charles immediately began issuing documents with the title of king, even though he had not yet dispossessed Manfred. Part of his preparations for invading the kingdom was the construction of alliances with the north Italian cities, which were largely autonomous at this time. On 11 September 1265, he appointed representatives to negotiate such alliances. Possible allies included the cities of Piacenza, Bologna and Parma, and in his letters his envoys were authorized 'to negotiate friendship, confederacy and alliance between our majesty, on the one hand, and the commune of the city of Piacenza [or Bologna or Parma], or those of that city who adhere to the party of the Church, on the other hand'. These documents show Charles carefully recruiting allies in north Italy and also, in these cases, recognizing that alliances might have to be made with a group or faction in the city – 'those of that city who adhere to the party of the Church'. The politics of thirteenth-century Italy thus clearly had a 'Church Party' in so many words. The documents, later bound into a register from a much later period, were identified and printed by Del Giudice in 1863, the source for the entry in Filangieri's 'reconstructed registers'.

The second example is quite different. It dates to much later in Charles' reign, when he was attempting to crush the rebellion against his rule in Sicily (the 'Sicilian Vespers'). Naval warfare was obviously central to this struggle, and on 17 May 1284 Charles ordered his vice-admiral to provide ships of various sizes to confront the rebels: thirty galleys, two galliots (small galleys) and three 'little boats'. This entry in the registers conveys information not only about the terminology used of ships and boats at this time but also of the specific features of these vessels: the galleys are to have 112 oars, the galliots 70 oars, the little boats 20 oars. It is only one small piece of evidence, but it can now be compared with others and a picture built up of seafaring in the Mediterranean in the thirteenth century. The reason this royal order is still accessible to us today is that, in the seventeenth century, Carlo de Lellis, a nobleman of the kingdom of Naples who devoted himself to genealogical work in the archives, made a note of it, and his manuscripts were deposited in the State Archive of

Naples in 1925. A few years after that, Filangieri published a volume containing the excerpts that de Lellis had made from the medieval chancery documents. Again, the seventeenth century had saved some of the Middle Ages for the twentieth century (compare the case of Helinand, discussed in Chapter 1 above).

The events of 1922 in Ireland and 1943 in Italy have much in common: in both cases the nineteenth-century bureaucratic state had created a central depository for public records, which was vulnerable to destruction in the chaos of twentieth-century war; in both cases there have been heroic efforts at reconstruction. A major difference, of course, is that the disaster of 1922 was a by-product of a military operation but that of 1943 was deliberate. Naturally there has been discussion of the motives behind such an act.

One historian who examined the events of 30 September 1943 in depth was the distinguished German medievalist Peter Herde. He had the unusual qualifications of being both a specialist in the history of the kingdom of Sicily in the Middle Ages and an experienced investigator in the archival sources of the Second World War, and his numerous publications range from a short book on Charles of Anjou, first of the line of Angevin rulers of the kingdom of Sicily, to a study of the Japanese occupation of south-east Asia in 1941–5. He had, moreover, personal experience of the upheavals of war. He was born in 1933, the year that Hitler came to power, in the small town of Ratibor in Silesia, at that time part of Germany. At the end of the Second World War, Poland was moved a hundred miles to the west, losing large areas in the east to the Soviet Union and gaining substantial territory in the west from Germany, including Silesia. Germans were expelled from these new territories, if they had not already fled from the advancing Red Army. Just before his twelfth birthday, Peter Herde's family joined this westward flight, resettling in a town in the Ruhr district of western Germany 562 miles (900 kilometres) from Ratibor (now renamed Racibórz).

In his research on the destruction of the Naples State Archive, Herde concentrated on the evidence provided on 6 February 1946 by Wolfgang Hagemann (1911–78), who had a leading role in the German army's 'Department for the Protection of Art' in Italy. On 1 October 1943 (so a day after the destruction of the Naples Archive), the German commander in Italy, Field Marshal Albert Kesselring, instructed Hagemann that 'within the limits imposed by military interests, everything conceivable should be done to protect the art and historical monuments in Italy'. Hagemann reported that, after news of the destruction of the Archive was published in an (unnamed) British magazine, he had been instructed to investigate the incident. He contacted the headquarters of the German 10th army, which at the time of the incident was in charge of the Nola region, where the Villa Montesano was located, and was informed that there was no record of any information about the State Archive of Naples, but that two villas in the region had been destroyed on 30 September as a reprisal for the killing of some German soldiers. Hagemann established that Filangieri had not informed the Germans of the presence of the Archive in the Villa Montesano, although he had written a letter explaining what it contained after the first appearance of the German soldiers at the Villa. This was shown to the soldiers, but it was probably not understood. Hagemann also wondered why Filangieri had never gone from his villa nearby to the Villa Montesano, either after hearing of the visits of German soldiers or when the fire had started. Herde's conclusion was expressed very clearly: 'One of the most significant archives of the West was destroyed. German blame for it cannot be disputed. The only question that arises is whether it was intentional or not; the latter is more probable.' He means that the archives were not the specific target, just the villa.

Filangieri was clearly stung by these criticisms. Indeed, he had not informed the German command about the presence of the archives, nor had he gone in person to the Villa Montesano (though one wonders what difference that would have made), but his position was complicated. Until four weeks before the destruction of the archives, Germans and Italians had been allies. German troops were stationed in Italy to support a joint defence against the Americans and British. The evacuation of the archives from Naples had been to protect them, not against marauding German soldiers, but against American and British bombing. The whirl of war can be very swift.

CHAPTER 9

Hanover, 9 October 1943:
The Ebstorf Map

A FEW WEEKS AFTER THE ARCHIVES OF NAPLES WERE incinerated by ravaging German troops, 500 Royal Air Force bombers were heading for Hanover. When the Second World War began, on 1 September 1939, aerial bombardment of enemy cities had been part of war for a generation. As early as the first week of August 1914, when the Germans invaded Belgium, their attack on Liège, their initial target, was supported by a Zeppelin dropping bombs on the city. It was not long before Zeppelins were carrying out bombing raids against British cities, including London, and later in the war they were joined by the huge Gotha bombers, some with a wing-span of over 77 feet (24 metres). This was the start of an unfinished story. In 1932, the Japanese were bombing Shanghai, and in 1937 Franco's German allies in the Spanish Civil War bombed the Basque town of Guernica, inspiring the most famous artistic depiction of aerial bombardment, Picasso's *Guernica*. Two years later, as Germany invaded Poland, and Britain and France declared war on Germany, starting the conflagration that would spread across the world, it was simply presumed that large-scale bombing of civilians would be coming soon. And it was.

In the night raid on Hanover of 9 October 1943, besides the 1,200 people blown to pieces or incinerated,

Figure 13. Hanover in 1945. Ullstein bild / Getty Images.

and the many more maimed, there was extensive physical destruction, especially through fire. A weather station in the centre of the city recorded a temperature increase between the hours of 2:00 and 4:00 a.m. from 10 degrees Celsius to 34 degrees (50 to 93 degrees Fahrenheit). Something that went up in flames that night was a map of the world made in the thirteenth or fourteenth century, the so-called Ebstorf World Map. The map was kept in the Central State Archive (*Hauptstaatsarchiv*) in Hanover, which was badly damaged. Along with the map, around 20 per cent of the documents in the archive were destroyed, including the records of the diocese of Hildesheim and the archbishopric

Figure 14. The Ebstorf Map. Heritage Images / Hulton Fine Art Collection / Getty Images.

of Bremen, which together amounted to well over 10,000 documents.

The Ebstorf Map is of a kind known as a *Mappa Mundi*, a Latin term meaning simply 'Map of the World' (the plural is *Mappae Mundi*). It is important to know what is meant by 'the World' here. Medieval people knew very well that the earth was a globe – 'God created the world completely round, in the same way that a ball is completely round', and, if there were no impediments, 'it would be possible for a man or an animal to go round the entire earth wherever they wished, like a fly going round an apple'. Map-makers and mariners (like Columbus) were thus aware that, if you sailed west from Spain, you would eventually come to Japan and China, although the distances involved made this a daunting prospect. This terrestrial globe was commonly described as divided horizontally into five zones, characterized by their climate: a northern arctic zone, a northern temperate zone, an equatorial torrid zone, a southern temperate zone and a southern antarctic zone. The usual (though not universal) belief was that the torrid zone was too hot for human beings to inhabit, or even to pass through. Hence, since human beings were created at one spot in the northern temperate zone (the Garden of Eden), they could never have reached the antipodes, which were thus habitable but not in fact inhabited. Since the arctic was also scarcely habitable, human beings could be found only in the northern temperate zone. Here, in this zone, as experience showed and time-honoured learning supported, was a habitable human world composed of three continents, Europe, Asia and Africa, linked by land. It was a widespread belief that the three continents had each been settled by descendants of one of the three sons of Noah (Shem, Ham and Japeth). This was the 'World' that the medieval world maps depicted: three continents, shading off to the frozen arctic in the north and the torrid spaces of Africa in the south, the whole land-mass surrounded by a circumambient ocean. A similar map of Eurasia and Africa could easily be produced today. The medieval *Mappa Mundi* thus depicts a segment of the globe. Such maps could be of various sizes. Some were in books and could obviously not show much detail, but others were planned as large wall maps. The Ebstorf Map was of the latter type and is the largest example known: it was made of 30 pieces of parchment, measured almost 12 feet by 12 feet (3.6 metres by 3.6 metres) overall, and was able to show 1,500 texts and 845 pictures.

The first mention of the map is in 1833, in a local Hanover newspaper, which alerted Georg Heinrich Wilhelm Blumenbach, a nobleman and official of the kingdom of Hanover, to the fact that 'some time before a map had been discovered in the archives of the convent of Ebstorf that was apparently of very great age' – Ebstorf is a small town about 60 miles (100 kilometres) north of Hanover. He investigated and found that 'some years earlier' the map had been found, covered in dust, in a chamber in the convent where sacred vessels, pictures of the Virgin Mary and similar things had been stored. It is possible that this collection of objects had been tucked away here at the time of the Reformation, when Ebstorf was transformed from a Catholic nunnery to a foundation for well-born Lutheran ladies. Because this chamber was affected by damp, it had been cleared out and the map discovered. The ladies of the convent unrolled it and hung it in their choir, where, unfortunately, 'an unknown evil-doer' had cut a piece out of it. Blumenbach published a description and discussion of the map in 1835, along with a lithographic drawing, explaining how he had come across it, giving an account of its contents, and asking where and when it was made, what sources were used and what its purpose was – deep and not easily answered questions. He concluded from the script that the map was from the thirteenth or

138

fourteenth century – something that is still believed – and pointed out features that suggested it might well have been produced in Ebstorf, where it was found. The same year, 1835, saw the foundation of the Historical Society of Lower Saxony (*Historischer Verein für Niedersachsen*), and the map was soon placed in its care (while remaining the property of the convent). The Society had premises in the State Archive in Hanover, which is how it came to be there.

The next important step in the investigation of the map occurred in 1891, when a photographic reproduction was published, with extensive annotation. This was edited by Ernst Sommerbrodt, headmaster of the *Gymnasium* (academic high school) in Lauban (now Lubań in Poland). The introduction to this volume explains the complex path from 'discovery' around 1830 to photographic reproduction in 1891: the issue of ownership, the financial support of the Prussian state (which had annexed Hanover in 1866), the technical complexities. The map had to be disassembled into its component sheets for the photography – no one knows what happened to the backing that held it together. Since not every parchment sheet required a whole photograph, the thirty original parchments were reproduced in twenty-five photographs, at half the size of the original. The results were not entirely satisfactory: the images were indistinct and many of the captions illegible. Sommerbrodt had to retouch the photographs with ink and, even then, much remained unclear. Despite all these reservations, this project of 1891 represented a big step towards protecting the object from oblivion. Today, copies of Sommerbrodt's book can be found as far from Ebstorf as the State Library of Victoria in

Melbourne, Australia. If our northern temperate zone suffers a catastrophe, a record of the Ebstorf Map will still survive.

In 1891, colour photography was in a purely experimental stage, so Sommerbrodt's reproduction showed simply shades of grey. But only a few years later an attempt was made to reproduce the colours of the map through lithography. This was part of the mammoth project of Konrad Miller, whose six-volume *Mappaemundi* was published between 1895 and 1898. He first commissioned a detailed drawing based on Sommerbrodt's photographs, which was then reduced in size to 30 per cent of the original, to meet the requirements of the lithographic process. It has been noted that the drawing appears to have clarified and 'improved' the photographs. Armed with this drawing, Miller visited the original map in Hanover and worked out a system whereby a palette of sixteen colours would give a good reproduction of every tint and shade on the map. This involved multiple lithographic stones and pressings. The end-result was a single-sheet coloured facsimile, more than 39 inches (1 metre) wide and tall, that was issued with volume V of Miller's *Mappaemundi*.

In 1930, another attempt was made to reproduce the map in colour. This was a hand-coloured facsimile based on Sommerbrodt's photographs and produced by August Kropp to celebrate the 75th anniversary of the Agricultural College (*Landbauschule*) in Ebstorf, where the facsimile is still displayed today. This later version can be compared with Miller's coloured reproduction, and differences between these two, coloured versions have been the subject of much debate and discussion. Obviously, analysis of the parchment, ink and paint of the original map is no longer possible, which is especially regrettable given the sophisticated tools and methods available today. For instance, in 2018, X-ray fluorescence was used to examine the chemical composition of the script and the images in the *Liber feudorum maior*, a book recording the texts of more than 900 charters that was put together on the orders of Alfonso II of Aragon (1162–96) and richly illustrated. Incorporating, but going beyond, stylistic analysis, the scientists identified the elements in the various pigments, such as the mercury in the vermilion and the lead in the white, and in this way built up a picture of the 'chromatic palette' associated with the different styles. Art historians had already distinguished earlier images of Romanesque type in the manuscript from those of the later Gothic type, but these were now shown to be clearly differentiated chemically. One ponders what the result of such an examination of the Ebstorf Map would have revealed. Later scientific developments are, sadly, irrelevant to an object that has been destroyed without trace. Investigation of the Ebstorf Map depends on the technology of reproduction available before 1943. Unless there is some miraculous discovery of new evidence, everything that will ever be known about the Ebstorf Map depends on what was recorded in the years 1833–1943, a window of opportunity of 110 years, now closed forever.

Like other maps of its kind, the Ebstorf World Map has east at the top and Jerusalem in the centre. The head of Christ appears at the apex, his hands at the right and left extremities and his feet at the bottom, so he is either embracing the world or the world is being identified with his body (this is by no means unique in such maps). There is a gradient in what is shown, from the familiar to the exotic, starting with Ebstorf itself, then the nearby Saxon towns, Lüneburg, Brunswick, Hanover, then more distant but quite well-known cities and regions, such as Aachen, Paris, Lombardy, before we come to remote lands like Libya and Babylon, finally reaching the edges of the world, where we find giants, men who know nothing of fire, cave-dwellers, people with ears so big they can use them as blankets and dog-headed men. Besides conveying geographical information, the map tells of biblical history: at the top there is the Garden of Eden, with Adam and Eve being tempted by the snake, in Jerusalem Christ is rising from the tomb. Both on the map and around it are numerous texts giving further information about places and animals. It is truly a visual encyclopaedia. But no one was going to use it to get somewhere.

There have now been almost two centuries of discussion of the date and place of origin of the map. The script has been dated anywhere from the first half of the thirteenth century to the second half of the fourteenth, though the balance of opinion tends to prefer 'around 1300'. Advocates of an early dating have included those who see a link between the map and Gervase of Tilbury, whose huge encyclopaedic work *Otia imperialia* was presented to the emperor Otto IV in 1215. The *Otia imperialia* is, in Gervase's own words, 'a description of the whole world' along with 'marvels of each province', and Gervase himself at one point refers to his book as a *Mappa Mundi*. Gervase, although presumably English by birth (Tilbury is in Essex, eastern England), was in the service of Otto IV in Provence, which was at that time part of the (Holy Roman) empire. Otto died in 1218. Scholars noticed that from 1223 to 1234 the provost, that is, the male cleric who supervised the nunnery of Ebstorf, bore the name Gervase. In addition, Ebstorf lay in the region where the Welf family had a dense concentration of estates, and Otto IV was a Welf. The theory thus developed that Gervase of Tilbury and Gervase the provost were the same man, and that he had been responsible either for the Ebstorf Map or for the model on which it was based. This is now a minority view. Although there are some texts on the map that are similar to certain parts of Gervase's *Otia*, these may simply have come from common sources, and any connection between Gervase and the map is now usually assumed to be of this general nature.

As mentioned, in 1835 Blumenbach suggested the map might have been made in Ebstorf itself. The evidence for this is quite strong. The cities of Brunswick and Lüneburg, both within 15 miles (25 kilometres) of Ebstorf, are given particular prominence on the map. Ebstorf itself, although hardly a significant site, is marked (and is clearly not a later addition, despite the occasional dissentient voice on this issue). Nearby there are three small rectangles with an inscription running through them 'here rest the blessed martyrs'. This reference to 'the blessed martyrs' is a pointer to local knowledge and may also help date the map. The 'martyrs' were, according to legend, a large group of northern German bishops and nobles who had been slaughtered by pagan Slavs in an earlier century and whose bodies were buried in four tombs in Ebstorf. Every year, on 1 August (the feast of St Peter in Chains), healing oil flowed from these tombs. There has been a complex, and confusing, debate among German scholars about when this legend first came into existence, since, if that could be dated, it would provide a terminus post quem for the map, but it is unlikely that consensus will be achieved. The earliest documentary reference to the martyrs is from 1419, when additional indulgences (spiritual benefits) were granted to those who visited Ebstorf 'out of reverence for the blessed martyrs resting at Ebstorf'. In any case, the marking of the tombs on the map strengthens the likelihood of its being produced in Ebstorf.

If the map was indeed produced at Ebstorf, it survived there for more than 500 years, an indication of the continuity of the institution, despite the Protestant Reformation. Unlike the situation in countries such as England and Scotland, where monasteries were dissolved, their buildings and libraries vandalized and their landed endowments seized, the Lutheran powers of northern Germany allowed such communities to continue, as long as they adopted the Lutheran form of Protestantism and submitted to the local rulers. Gradually, the traces of monastic life in these foundations were diluted or disappeared. In Ebstorf, the use of Latin for services was abandoned by 1619, along with prayers for the dead and the *Ave Maria*, common dining ceased by 1692 and in the eighteenth century the ladies of the community had their own dwellings within the foundation. By the time of the rediscovery of the Ebstorf Map, the community consisted of fifteen noble ladies headed by an abbess. The medieval community of Benedictine nuns thus became a community of pious Lutheran ladies without the loss of its property or archives. This is why the foundation is so rich in medieval documents: there are 626 of them, of which 441 are originals, not later copies. Most of these are still in Ebstorf; it was only those that, for some reason, found their way to the State Archive in Hanover that suffered losses in the raid of October 1943. If only the map had been kept in Ebstorf! There were indeed, after the war, complaints that the evacuation of the documents in the Archive had started too late and had not concentrated on the most important historical materials. This is not an implausible point of view. The Archive had already suffered bomb damage in July and September of 1943, so the risk was clear.

The destruction of the Ebstorf Map means that the only surviving *Mappa Mundi* of any comparable size is now the Hereford *Mappa Mundi* in Hereford cathedral. The Hereford Map gives an idea of what was lost, although it is considerably smaller than the Ebstorf Map (4 feet 5 inches by 5 feet 5 inches, or 1.35 metres by 1.65 metres) and made of a single calf skin, not thirty. This explains the difference in the shape of the two maps: the Hereford Map uses the area of the calf's neck, giving an elongated area of parchment at the top, while the Ebstorf map has trimmed its thirty pieces of parchment to produce a purely rectangular shape. Both the Hereford and Ebstorf Maps have east at the top, Jerusalem at the centre, with Asia occupying the upper half of the map, Europe and Africa the lower half. All of this is quite standard. The Bible stories, the strange peoples, the pictures of towns, all this is common to both. But we can know much more about the Hereford Map, since it still exists.

The origin of the Hereford Map has to be deduced from the object itself. As is the case also with *Beowulf* (above, Chapter 4), there is no medieval mention of the map, the first reference dating to 1684. A late eighteenth-century drawing shows the wooden case in which the map was displayed: it was a triptych, with folding shutters which were decorated with the figures of the angel Gabriel and the Virgin Mary at the Annunciation. By 1805, however, these side panels were no longer attached to the case and their later (and present) whereabouts are unknown, if they still exist. The original back panel, made of six oak planks, was also later mislaid, but only temporarily, from 1948 to 1989, when it turned up in the former cathedral stables.

Since the Hereford Map is still physically present, we can see details no longer in existence on the Ebstorf Map, for example the holes made by the compass when circles were drawn. And, because the Hereford Map, unlike the Ebstorf Map, survived into a time when ever more sophisticated techniques of scientific analysis have become available, research into its dating and physical composition can be undertaken based on more than the style of its handwriting and imagery. Particularly useful in this respect was the surviving medieval panel that formed the back of the case in which the map was housed and which was rediscovered in 1989. In 2004, the dean and chapter of Hereford commissioned a dendrochronological (tree-ring) analysis of this panel by Ian Tyers, who concluded that the trees from which the oak boards came must have been felled in the period 1289–1311. This fits in extremely well with the expert opinions of Malcolm Parkes on the date of the handwriting on the map (c. 1290–1310) and Nigel Morgan on the style of the illustrations (c. 1285–1300).

Complicating the story is an inscription at the bottom left of the parchment, asking that all who see the map should pray for 'Richard of Haldingham or of Lafford who made it and laid it out'. Haldingham and Lafford are two places in Lincolnshire, now known as Holdingham and Sleaford. Holdingham is (or was) a hamlet, but Sleaford was a parish, a borough and – under the name Lafford – a prebend of Lincoln cathedral, held by a canon. The records of Lincoln cathedral show that from 1265 to 1278 there was a canon called Richard ('Richard de Bello') who is identified in 1277 as 'Master Richard de Bello, treasurer of Lincoln and prebendary of Lafford', the title 'Master' indicating a high level of education. Since this Richard de Bello could quite reasonably describe himself also as 'Richard of Lafford', some scholars have seen in him the creator either of the map or of an earlier model for the map. A second, younger Richard de Bello, who was a canon of Hereford 1305–26, has also been brought into the discussion, especially since the dating of the map from the dendrochronological analysis would make its association with the other Richard less plausible. Understandably, there are champions of both Hereford and Lincoln as the place of origin of the map. Whoever was responsible for the map, and however proud they could justifiably be about its beauty, they must have been dismayed when it was pointed out to them that they had labelled Europe 'Africa' and Africa 'Europe'!

The Hereford Map was only one of several in thirteenth-century England. In 1239, Henry III ordered a *Mappa Mundi* to be painted in the hall of the royal castle at Winchester, and there was another in his chamber in Westminster Palace. The monk, historian and artist Matthew Paris (d. 1259) produced a simplified and book-size *Mappa Mundi* that, he explained, he had based on others, one by Master Robert of *Melekeleia* and another in Waltham abbey. Whether these were wall maps or maps in books is not stated. Robert of Melkley sounds English and shares his rare name with Gervase of Melkley, who wrote a handbook on poetry and an epitaph for William Marshal, who was regent of England in the first years of Henry III's reign. Another late thirteenth-century English *Mappa Mundi* survives only in part. This is the 'Duchy of Cornwall Map' (so-called because it is in the Duchy of Cornwall Office in London), a section of 24.4 inches by 20.9 inches (62 centimetres by 53 centimetres) representing the lower right-hand part of a map that must have originally been about 5 feet 3 inches (1.64 metres) square, so quite comparable with the Hereford Map in size. There is also the 'Psalter Map', a *Mappa Mundi* incorporated in a psalter, dateable to after 1262, and now in the British Library (Add MS 28681); it is 7 inches by 5 inches (17 centimetres x 12.5 centimetres), so considerably smaller than a sheet of modern A4.

It is clear that all these maps have a strong family resemblance and must descend in some way from a common predecessor. For example, on both the Ebstorf and the Hereford Maps, the southern rim of Africa is shown as inhabited by monstrous peoples. These usually have labels: 'a people who have mouths fused together and draw nourishment through a little opening with straws' (Ebstorf), 'a people whose mouth is fused together; they feed through a straw' (Hereford), both illustrated by a man drinking with a straw; 'the Mauretanian Ethiopians have four eyes' (Ebstorf), 'the Marmini Ethiopians have fourfold eyes' (Hereford); 'there are Hymandropeds, always falling forwards, as it were' (Ebstorf),

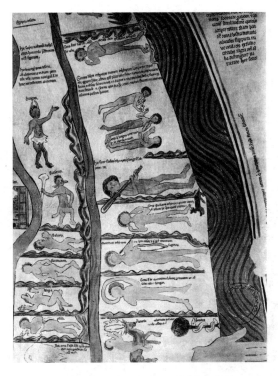

Figure 15. The Ebstorf Map – Detail of the southern rim of Africa inhabited by monstrous peoples. Alamy Images.

'the Himatopodes creep rather than walk with fluid movements of their legs, proceeding more by gliding than stepping' (Hereford). There are many such similarities between the Ebstorf and Hereford Maps, and with the other surviving *Mappae Mundi*, but always with sufficient differences to suggest that maps of this type had been circulating and being copied for many years, with changes and sometimes misinterpretations creeping in.

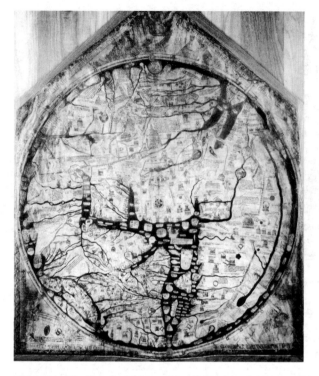

Figure 16. The Hereford *Mappa Mundi*. De Agostini Picture Library / Getty Images.

A great deal of scholarly work has gone into exploring and identifying the sources of these maps. Just as in the case of *The Garden of Delights*, much of the information they display goes back to the encyclopaedias of the Roman empire and to the simplified versions and adaptations of them that were produced in the early Middle Ages. The Hymantopodes, for instance, creeping along, are found in the geographical work of Pomponius Mela and in Pliny's *Natural History*, a huge

150

compendium of natural science and lore, both of which date
to the first century AD; two centuries later they were taken up
by Solinus, the abbreviator of Pliny, whose work was popular
and familiar throughout the Middle Ages. The description of
Hymantopodes on the Hereford Map is identical to that in
Solinus. Similar literary trails can be traced for scores of
entries on these maps. The fusion of these textual sources
with an actual map – a pictorial representation of the known
world – had certainly taken place by the eighth century, when
there are surviving examples in books. It has also been argued
that the twelfth-century theologian Hugh of St Victor gave
a great impetus to map production. His *Description of
a Mappa Mundi* begins, 'Wise men, learned in both secular
and ecclesiastical letters, are accustomed to depict the world
on a board or skin, so they can show, to those who wish to
know unknown things, the images of things, since they cannot
display the things themselves.' Although he asserted that he
was more interested in the spiritual significance of maps, he
nevertheless did discuss such things as labelling, colours and
so on. He describes the monstrous peoples of Ethiopia,
including those who have no mouth and have to drink
through straws.

Already at the time of the creation of the Ebstorf and
Hereford Maps, entirely new kinds of cartography were devel-
oping. Two were of particular importance: the Portolan maps
and the maps based on the newly rediscovered work of the
ancient geographer Ptolemy. Unlike the Ebstorf and Hereford
Maps, Portolans could actually be used to get you somewhere,
since they were produced by and for mariners in the
Mediterranean and showed sea-routes and coastlines.

A network of lines connected the different points along the coasts, and the maps had compass roses and wind directions. The accuracy of the coastlines is remarkable, with dozens of coastal settlements named, though the inland areas are often blank, being of no use to seafarers. Portolans became common in the fourteenth and fifteenth centuries, just as knowledge of Ptolemy revived. This important astronomer and geographer had worked in Alexandria, a great centre of Greek scientific learning, in the second century AD, and had produced a *Geography* that gave the coordinates of latitude and longitude for more than 6,000 places. Latitude was measured from the equator and could be established quite well by astronomical instruments, notably the astrolabe, while longitude was measured from the Fortunate Isles, the westernmost point of the known world, and was trickier to establish (a problem not finally solved until the eighteenth century). If these places were plotted on a flat surface of parchment or paper, and supplemented by travellers' reports of distances and so forth, a remarkably accurate map could be produced. Ptolemy's original work included twenty-six maps of Eurasia and north Africa. The text and maps of the *Geography* were scarcely known for most of the Middle Ages, but around 1300 a copy was identified in Byzantium, and was studied and copied by Byzantine scholars, who brought the work to the West around a century later. A copy reached Florence in 1397, a Latin translation appeared soon after that and finally a printed edition was produced in 1475.

These Portolans and Ptolemaic maps were the maps that Columbus would have known – he himself made Portolans. And with Columbus and his voyage of 1492 there began a new age in cartography and geography (as also in the history of the world). As Europeans spread across the globe, one thing they never came across were people with no mouths, people with four eyes or Hymantopodes. The old monsters at the edge of the world disappeared from geography and moved into legend and fiction. At the same time, Europeans encountered humans who were completely unknown to their prior thinking and view of the world, and they had to find some way to integrate them into the history of humanity, which they did in various ways, but always within a biblical framework. Eventually the world was mapped, revealed as containing entire continents that the *Mappae Mundi* had not shown. Medieval cartography became a subject for specialist scholarly investigation, often tinged with condescension. A classic survey of medieval geographical know-ledge, published in 1925, turned to medieval maps with what sounds like a sigh: 'Their bright colors, naïve legends, childlike but often skillfully drawn vignettes, and preposterous inaccuracy take us back into the atmosphere of a credulous and uncrit-ical age.'

The Ebstorf Map and the Hereford Map, both prob-ably produced around 1300, were the high point of the *Mappa Mundi* tradition: large, public representations of the world as imagined by contemporaries – a world that was full, strange and wonderful, and shaped by divine providence. The nuns of Ebstorf and the canons of Hereford doubtless regarded their maps as one of the greatest treasures of their churches. Of course, the biggest difference between the Ebstorf Map and the Hereford Map is that the former no longer exists. In his guide book of 1955, the Reverend A. L. Moir reported that, during the Second World War, the Hereford *Mappa Mundi* was sent for safekeeping, first to the wine cellar of Hampton Court Castle in the countryside 10 miles (16 kilometres) north of Hereford and subsequently to a coal mine at Bradford-on-Avon in Wiltshire (it seems that there is no coal mine at Bradford-on-Avon, though there are numerous underground stone workings, one of which was used as a bomb shelter). One wonders why similar protective measures were not undertaken in the case of the Ebstorf Map, especially since Hanover had been bombed on several occasions before the raid of 9 October 1943. When the Hereford *Mappa Mundi* was restored in the late 1940s, it was – deeply ironically – placed in a new case built out of wood from the City of London churches that had been bombed in the war. Aerial warfare and medieval world maps intersected again.

CHAPTER 10

Chartres, 26 May 1944:
The Municipal Library

I N THE LATE 1880S, TWO LEARNED FRENCH SCHOLARS, Auguste Molinier and Henri Omont, were busy cataloguing the manuscripts of the Municipal Library of Chartres. Both of them were graduates of the distinguished 'Charter School' (*Ecole des Chartes*), a state institution which had been established in Paris in 1821 to give a solid grounding in medieval Latin and palaeography to future archivists and librarians. Chartres had a large and important collection, with 551 manuscript volumes earlier than 1500. Given their expertise, Molinier and Omont concentrated on these medieval books, recording a brief account of their contents, details of their size, probable date and their place of origin prior to coming to the Municipal Library. Most of these books had previously belonged to churches and monasteries in Chartres, which had been nationalized in 1790 in the early days of the French Revolution. Chartres cathedral, which had been converted into a 'Temple of Reason' in the revolutionary period, had contributed the largest number of volumes (almost 60 per cent), although eleven of the most precious, including a very rare fifth-century book, had been spirited away to the National Library in Paris. The results of the labours of Molinier and Omont, and of their collaborators who worked on more modern manuscripts, were published in

1890 in a substantial volume of almost 600 pages, as part of a massive project, the *General Catalogue of the Manuscripts of the Public Libraries of France*. It is a particularly valuable piece of work, since almost all the manuscripts described in it were annihilated or reduced to charred fragments in 1944.

In the weeks leading up to the Allied landings in Normandy on 6 June 1944 – 'D-Day' – an intense air campaign was launched by British and American forces, designed to disrupt and destroy the infrastructure on which the occupying German troops in France depended. Many of the targets were railways, bridges and other crucial elements of the communications network, but another priority, as defined in General Eisenhower's directive of 17 April 1944, was 'to deplete the German air force and particularly the German fighter forces, and to destroy and disorganize the facilities supporting them'. This naturally included airfields. An added complication was the need to select targets in such a way that it did not spell out the Allies' planned invasion sites. There was an airfield at Chartres, and this was chosen as one target among many.

There is some disagreement about the exact course of events during the bombing raid on Chartres on 26 May, though the basic outline – and the consequences – are clear. The website of the American Air Museum contains the following account, starting with a reference to a B26 'Marauder' with code number 42–96199:

> 42–96199 took off from station 162 Chipping Ongar, Essex, UK, on a mission to bomb Chartres' airfield. Around 17.55, just as the plane, part of the first bombing group, was

starting its run, a flak barrage scored a direct hit on the No. 2 engine. The latter plummeted free of the aircraft and landed near the town church. The plane itself went into a slow dive. The pilot dropped both 900 kg bombs in order to free the bay door for a potential bail out. The rest of the group thought it to be the attack signal and dropped theirs as well. The damage caused was enormous, killing about 50 civilians and setting the town library on fire.

The account continues, stating that three of the six-man crew of 42–96199 bailed out, and soon became prisoners of war, but the other three died as the plane crashed into the ground.

The historian of Chartres, Roger Joly (1924–2002), actually interviewed the two surviving members of the crew of 42–96199 in 1995. Bob Smith, the pilot, and Walter Wright, the navigator, confirmed that their target was the airfield, that the right engine of their plane was knocked out by anti-aircraft fire and that they had to drop their bombs, since the bomb bay was their route for bailing out of the plane. So far, all this fits with the account of the American Air Museum (indeed, the crew members may well have been the source of that account too). What Roger Joly found unconvincing was the idea that the two bombs from 42–96199 had fallen in the region of the Municipal Library and that this had been taken as a signal to drop their bombs by the other planes in the formation. He could back up his points by detailed local knowledge and concluded that 'the bombing must, without a doubt, be considered the result of an error of judgment made by the commander of the formation'. Whether we credit Joly's view or the other is not an essential matter, since both explain the bombing of the centre of Chartres as the result of a mistake, and there is no doubt either about who carried it out – the American 387th Bomb Group, based at the time in Chipping Ongar – or about the results – fifty deaths and the destruction of the library.

The raid on Chartres illustrates the moral complexities of bombing occupied countries rather than enemy countries. It was impossible to target with such precision that no French civilian casualties occurred, and one estimate is that about 6,000 French civilians died as a result of the pre-invasion bombing (total civilian deaths from Allied bombing throughout France in March to May 1944 were well over 15,000). One of the pilots flying a Spitfire in support of American bombers in a raid on Rouen, the chief city of Normandy, was a member of the Free French forces and reported staring down at the railyards, the target of the raid, still undamaged, while hundreds of houses were in flames. He wrote, 'How many of my fellow Frenchmen – all civilians – had died or would die for nothing, before our eyes ... I started yelling over the radio, "You American sons of bitches!"' Joly reports that he had seen photos of the ruins of the centre of Chartres taken by an inhabitant of the city, which the photographer had prefaced by a plate reading (in French), 'Another crime of the Anglo-Americans!'

Air raids on Chartres were foreseen from well before the outbreak of the war, and preparations made to ensure the safety of the artistic and literary treasures of the city. Between 25 August and 4 September 1939, the irreplaceable stained-glass windows in the cathedral, which date to the twelfth and thirteenth centuries, were packed into more than 900 crates and placed in the crypt. When the Germans advanced into France in the spring of 1940, most of these were shipped off to the protection of the underground chambers below the castle of Fongrenon in the Perigord, 240 miles (385 kilometres) to the south. This is why these superb images in glass can still be seen by tourists, scholars and worshippers today. At the same time, similar measures were taken to protect the hundreds of medieval manuscripts in the Municipal Library. On 5 September 1939, two days after the French declared war, the manuscripts, along with the early printed books and other valuable volumes, were taken in crates to the Château de Villebon, 14 miles (23 kilometres) from Chartres. After the surrender of France in June 1940, a German officer visited the library in Chartres to confiscate any volumes that were on the list of prohibited books issued by the German occupying forces, while a group of German soldiers, suspicious of the crates in the Château de Villebon, opened a few of them but left after finding they contained just books (a very different outcome from that at the Montesano Villa).

However, later that year, on 3 December 1940, Dr Ernst Wermke, head of the 'Library Protection Division' of the occupying German forces, arrived at the Municipal Library, and he ordered the manuscripts and other books at the Château de Villebon to be returned to the library in Chartres. Wermke, who was Director of the Municipal Library in Breslau (now Wrocław), had written a doctoral thesis on the thirteenth-century Church and compiled the standard bibliography of the history of East and West Prussia. After the war, he wrote a memoir of his experiences in 'protecting' French libraries (the typescript is now in the State Library in Berlin). There is also relevant evidence in the official report of Hermann Fuchs on the activities of the Library Protection Division in France, dated 20 September 1944, in which he explained that books could be brought back from their places of safety to their original location if the Division required it. As a recent scholar pointed out, 'Fuchs himself admitted that in this way the Division was to blame for the destruction of the Municipal Library in Chartres in a British air-raid of 26 May 1944' (the raid was of course American, although launched from British bases).

Figure 17. The archivist and pioneer of aerial photography at Chartres, Maurice Jusselin. Arch. dép. D'Eure-et-Loir, 10 Fi 72–04.

There is no doubt that the return of the manuscripts to Chartres was commanded by Wermke, since the relevant orders have been published, but the motive is more a matter of interpretation. An important source for these events is the history of the Municipal Library published by Maurice Jusselin in 1962. Jusselin (1882–1964) was the archivist in charge of the archives of the département of Eure-et-Loir, which includes Chartres, and was personally involved in the affairs of the library, organizing a major exhibition there in February 1942, which displayed the treasures of the library, including illuminated medieval manuscripts, and drew crowds to Chartres. The exhibition catalogue is an important record predating the bombing. Jusselin's interpretation of Wermke's instruction to move the manuscripts back to the city is as follows:

> The situation was that of a country that had been invaded. The message that the German authorities wish to impose is that everything is going for the best under their protection, that nothing prevents France from resuming all its activities without any concerns, and that the local precautionary measures taken before the invasion ought to be revoked. The Wehrmacht and the Luftwaffe are there to avert danger. The Library, reincorporating the deposit at Villebon, ought to be available in its entirety just as it was before 1940 and this without delay.

Of course, Jusselin's view here is speculation but not implausible.

Jusselin's work over many decades was important in preserving knowledge of the Chartres manuscripts prior to their destruction. He edited some texts, wrote a survey of the liturgical manuscripts, and, as a passionate photographer, took photographs of some of them. He combined his love of photography with a love of aviation – he served in that branch during the First World War – and secured the first aerial views of Chartres cathedral in the years before that war. His collection of more than 1,700 photographs is now in the Chartres Library. Many show the early days of the Chartres airfield, clearly a site of fascination for Jusselin, and it is poignant to reflect that it was the existence of this target that led, however indirectly, to the destruction of the library.

What was destroyed in Chartres in May 1944 was a library, not an archive. The Municipal Library of Chartres did not house hundreds of years of governmental documents, as the Public Record Office of Ireland and the State Archive of Naples did. It was a collection of books, and had been formed through the acquisition of books from other collections – as far as the medieval manuscripts are concerned, from the libraries of the great churches of Chartres: the cathedral, the Benedictine monastery of Saint-Père-en-Vallée and, to a lesser degree, the Augustinian canons of Saint-Jean-en-Vallée, the Dominicans and the abbey of Notre-Dame de Josaphat. When these religious establishments were abolished during the French Revolution, their assets, including books, were transferred to the state. So, the collection of books in the Municipal Library in 1890 was like an archaeological deposit whose contents have been washed down by various streams. Like many libraries, it was a library of libraries. However, although the medieval manuscripts that Omont and Molinier catalogued do not represent any one single medieval collection, they nevertheless give a very good idea of the nature of medieval Christian ecclesiastical culture, its different components and its development over time.

The chart below shows the composition of the medieval collection in the library in 1890, sorted by type of text and by date of manuscript. The following categories have been used:

- biblical texts and (post-patristic) biblical commentaries
- liturgy, including commentaries on the liturgy and Books of Hours
- patristic texts, that is, writings of the Church Fathers of the formative centuries of Christianity (c. 100–600)
- law, both canon (that is, Church law, including conciliar decrees) and Roman Law
- the 'Arts': grammar; rhetoric; logic; arithmetic; astronomy; music; geometry
- theology not covered in the previous categories
- medicine
- saints' Lives
- sermons (post-patristic)
- history.

(Administrative documents and categories with only a few items have not been included.)

Century	Biblical	Liturgical	Patristic	Legal	Arts	Theology	Medicine	Sts' Lives	Sermons	History
9th	5	1	25	1	3		1			2
10th	7	2	13	2	13	1	2			1
11th	6	3	5	2	8		1	2		2
12th	29	9	30	1	8	2	3	6	4	1
13th	47	19	2	16	1	13	2	7		
14th	14	28	2	47	5	12	10	8	4	1
15th	1	39	1	4	1	2	3			2

Some patterns emerge at first glance: the large number of biblical texts and commentaries from the twelfth, thirteenth and (to a lesser degree) fourteenth centuries (a number that is so high partly because it includes a nineteen-volume Bible of the thirteenth century from the Dominican convent and a seven-volume set of biblical commentary of the fourteenth century from the cathedral); the large and increasing number of liturgical texts (especially Hours) over the last three medieval centuries; the cluster of patristic texts in the ninth and the twelfth centuries; the boom in law books after 1200. Such patterns can be tied to wider trends, for example the revival of legal learning that began around 1100 and led to the codification of Church law in the decretals (a collection of papal decrees) of 1234, the renewal of Roman Law and the teaching of both laws in the universities that arose in the twelfth and thirteenth centuries. The manuscripts from Chartres include Roman Law texts, such as the Code and the Digest, as well as commentaries upon them. The Digest, part of the codification of Roman Law undertaken by the emperor Justinian in the sixth century, is an example of a text that was virtually unknown in the early Middle Ages, until a manuscript turned up in Italy in the eleventh century, allowing copies to be made and the Digest to become a central text of medieval learned law. By far the greatest number of legal manuscripts in Chartres, however, were texts of the papal decretals and commentaries on the decretals, reflecting the sophistication and pervasiveness of the legal culture of the late medieval Church. Other patterns can be explained by different considerations. Liturgical books, for example, which were subject to everyday use, would need replacing fairly regularly, so it is not surprising that the bulk of them are late medieval. There are some noteworthy gaps in the collection – remarkably, there is only a single example of ancient Roman literature, Ovid's *Metamorphoses* (MS 200), from the late thirteenth century, preserved at Saint-Père.

The cluster of ninth-century patristic texts – roughly half from the cathedral, half from Saint-Père – represents the activity of the so-called Carolingian Renaissance, when older texts were copied out in the characteristic script known as 'Caroline miniscule' or 'Carolingian minuscule', a regular, uniform style that spread across western Europe and indeed is the ancestor of modern book type, such as this one. The ninth-century patristic collection at Chartres had works by Ambrose (d. 397), Jerome (d. 419), Augustine (d. 430), Cassiodorus (d. c. 580) and Gregory the Great (d. 604), all the main figures of the early Latin Church, as well as a single work by the Greek theologian Origen (d. 253), his exegesis of the Old Testament Books of Numbers and Leviticus (MS 101). Origen composed this in Caesarea in Palestine in the 230s or 240s, writing in his native Greek, and, while the original Greek version does not survive, a Latin translation was made in Italy by the monk Rufinus in the years 400–10, and in the following century a copy of this came into the hands of Cassiodorus (just mentioned). All subsequent manuscripts, including that at Chartres, are copies, or copies of copies, of Cassiodorus' book. In this way, a Greek work composed in Palestine in the third century, translated into Latin in the fifth and copied, in its Latin version, in France in the ninth, survived the centuries, including both Reformation and Revolution, until 1944 – 1,700 years after its composition.

There was no university at Chartres in the Middle Ages, perhaps because the city lay between Paris, the most important university north of the Alps, which was around 50 miles (80 kilometres) away, and the significant University of Orléans, which was even nearer. However, in the period before universities took shape, which they did from around 1200, there were many centres with a reputation for study and teaching, and Chartres was one of them. Fulbert, bishop of Chartres 1006–28, composed letters, sermons and poems, and had many students, who preserved warm memories of their time at 'the Chartres academy', as they called it. A century later, Bernard of Chartres, who was chancellor of Chartres and died in 1124, was also evidently a famous and respected teacher. His reputation is attested especially in the words of John of Salisbury, a companion of Thomas Becket and bishop of Chartres 1176–80, who had studied in France in the years 1136–47 and presumably met former students of Bernard's then. John discusses Bernard's approach to teaching and some of his specific doctrines. He praises Bernard as 'Bernard of Chartres, the most abundantly flowing fountain of letters in Gaul in modern times' and goes into some detail about his teaching method, which involved pointing out the grammatical, rhetorical and logical features of the text being studied and requiring students to memorize large bodies of verse and prose, as well as composing something every day. Bernard always took into account 'the capacity of his audience'. John writes, 'As old Bernard of Chartres frequently used to propound to his listeners, there are three kinds of natural intellectual capacity: one that flies, one that is very low and one that is between these two' – as is usual in these trinities, the middle course is to be preferred. He urged on some by exhortation, some by the rod. John calls Bernard 'the most perfect Platonist of our time' and reports that he put a great deal of effort in attempting to reconcile the philosophies of Plato and Aristotle (something no one has ever achieved). Bernard's respect for the ancients was balanced by a sense that thinkers of his own time could go beyond them, thanks to their efforts: 'Bernard of Chartres used to say that we are like dwarves sitting on the shoulders of giants, so that we are able to see more and further than them, not by our own sharpness of vision or bodily magnitude, but because we are raised aloft and elevated by their gigantic stature.'

A two-volume work in the Chartres library, the *Heptateucon* of Thierry of Chartres (MSS 497–8), contained a full (though probably ideal) syllabus of the 'Arts' education of the time. Although all that now exists are sad fragments, a full microfilm of the two manuscripts was made before the war. *Heptateucon* means 'Seven Books', and the two volumes contain seven sections, each dealing with one of the Seven Liberal Arts. The text is an anthology of the classical authorities on each of these arts, so the section on grammar consists of excerpts from Donatus and Priscian, grammarians who had worked in the later centuries of the Roman empire, the section on rhetoric is made up of quotations from Cicero (or works attributed to him) and so forth. Thierry was chancellor of Chartres from 1141 until his death in 1151, and he bequeathed fifty volumes, including these two, to the cathedral. Since the Seven Liberal Arts are represented in stone carvings on the twelfth-century Royal Portal of Chartres cathedral, Thierry must have seen them daily.

Figure 18a. Surviving fragments of Thierry of Chartres' *Heptateucon.*
Chartres, Bibliothèque municipal, MS 497, fol. 39. Picture: IRHT-CNRS.

The vast majority of the manuscripts preserved in the library are on parchment and in Latin, the general language of the learned class. Only thirteen of are paper (two of these only in part), reflecting the great preponderance in the Chartres collection of books produced before 1400, the time when paper began to be more common in north-western Europe (in northern France only 5 per cent of fourteenth-century

Figure 18b. Surviving fragments of Thierry of Chartres' *Heptateucon*. Chartres, Bibliothèque municipal, MS 497, fol. 39v. Picture: IRHT-CNRS.

manuscripts are paper, while in the fifteenth century the figure is 45 per cent). The oldest paper manuscript in the library, MS 233, is explicitly dated 1355. There are a small number of texts in French: 22 volumes of the 551 contain material in that language, the largest category being Books of Hours of the fifteenth century. One of these (MS 543), we know, was made in 1478 for the wife of a resident of Chartres (inside it she offered a reward for the return of the book if it was lost), and it is likely that several of these Books of Hours were originally made for lay patrons before finding their way to the cathedral library. Other texts in French include, rather unusually, a translation of a handbook of canon law proced-ure, two copies of the *Somme le Roi*, which was a guide to the virtues and vices written for Philip III in 1279, some sermons, allegorical poems, and two Rules for religious communities of women.

There is one volume in French with an entirely local focus (MS 1027), containing an account of the miracles of the Virgin of Chartres, as well as a chronicle. Chartres cathedral claimed to possess the chemise that the Virgin Mary had been wearing when she gave birth to Christ, and consequently Mary loved Chartres especially and 'had chosen that church as her special home on earth'. This was manifested in the miracles that were experienced by pilgrims coming to her church or those who invoked her help, who were cured of illness, saved from danger or even brought back to life. On one occasion the 11-year-old son of a servant in the castle of Sully-sur-Loire fell into the moat and, when found, was deemed to be dead. But the lady of the castle, who was the boy's godmother, ran up and invoked the Virgin, 'the glorious lady of Chartres' (so, lady appealing to lady), and ordered the boy to be suspended upside down. A vast quantity of water poured out of him, he revived, and the lady of Sully was sure to visit Chartres cathedral every year with thanks and gifts. Another time, a knight from Aquitaine, who was involved in a lethal feud with his enemies, came to Chartres, bringing with him several chemises or shirts, which he pressed up against the shrine where the Virgin's chemise was kept, and, on return to Aquitaine, he always wore one of these. His enemies managed to ambush him when he was unarmed, but they found their lances could not penetrate the shirt he was wearing. These miracles were all recorded in Latin, probably by a canon of Chartres, in the first half of the thirteenth century, and it was this text that was translated into French verse in the middle years of that century by Master Jean Le Marchant, 'so that lay people can understand it'.

The very small number of books in French is noteworthy, given the flourishing of vernacular writing in the later centuries of the Middle Ages. The different European languages enter the written record at different periods. Some vernaculars did leave written material in the early Middle Ages, like Irish or Old English, with inscriptions from pre-Christian times and written documents from the seventh or eighth centuries, but it is only from the twelfth century that a really significant increase in the amount written in the vernacular begins. Latin and Greek have a continuous history from ancient times, and Latin was the predominant written language in the West throughout the early and central Middle Ages, being slowly joined and then matched by the vernacular languages. In the case of the Romance languages, those descended from Latin, it is difficult to draw a sharp line between mother and daughter tongues: it is hard to say when the everyday spoken Latin (as distinct from the language of books) turned into early French or early Spanish or early Italian. One wonders how much Latin and how much French was spoken in Chartres cathedral in the medieval centuries.

The manuscripts sometimes reveal something of their history and the individuals involved with them. Scribes might write their names in the manuscripts they copied. The ninth-century scribe Amalbertus seized the chance to show off, making the following note in Greek letters: 'Here ends Book Fifteen, happily. God be praised. Amen. It is finished. Amalbertus made me. This ending is great joy.' Such expressions of relief at finishing the job are quite common. The scribe of a thirteenth-century copy of a work by the Dominican William Peraldus wrote, 'Here ends the *Summa*, here this book ends, may the scribe be free of reproach. It ends, it should end, let the scribe go and play.' In a tenth-century manuscript from Saint-Père of the ancient Jewish historian Josephus, the scribe has either drawn or commissioned a self-portrait, a figure writing on a lectern, inscribed with his name – 'Robert' (MS 29, fol. 244v). A ninth-century copy of Pseudo-Jerome's treatise on the Psalms not only contains the name of the scribe – 'you who read, pray for the scribe, Dodaldus the clerk, if you wish to have the Lord as your protector' – but also the circumstances of its arrival in the cathedral collection: 'Richulfus offered this book, through the hands of Giselbertus, bishop of the church of St Mary of Chartres.' Giselbertus was bishop of Chartres in the years 859–78, while Dodaldus has been identified as a gifted cleric of the church of Tours working in the early years of the ninth century – Tours was a particularly important centre of book production in the Carolingian period.

Spaces in the manuscripts might be used for jottings or short notes over the years. For instance, in a thirteenth-century copy of biblical commentaries by the theologian

Figure 19. The scribe Robert in Chartres MS 29. Chartres, Bibliothèque municipal, MS 29, fol. 244v. Picture: IRHT-CNRS.

William of Auvergne, there is a note (in French) about the battle of Bouvines in 1214 ('in 1214 count Ferrand [of Flanders] went to war against the king'), while another reader recorded on the fly-leaf, 'In the year of the Lord 1254, on the Sunday when "Reminiscere" is sung, we made an inventory of the goods of the church' (this gives a precise date of 8 March 1254).

In a fourteenth-century manuscript of the *Derivationes* of Huguccio of Pisa (a Latin lexicon) someone has written (in Latin verse), 'In the year one thousand three hundred and twelve, as the sun was setting, the earth shuddered and groaned.' As well as incidents such as these – battles, Church business and earthquakes – the occasional blank piece of parchment could be used for recipes. A ninth-century manuscript of Gregory the Great's commentary on Ezechiel has a short addition, in an eleventh-century hand, giving a remedy for migraine, beginning 'Peony root cooked in very old rose oil'. Such an odd discrepancy between the text and the added material is also found in a thirteenth-century manuscript of canon law, to which has been added a charm to procure a swift childbirth, which 'has been proved to be true by me, Ralph de Verdu'. This volume was one of eleven given to the cathedral by William of St-Benigne, a canon of Chartres, in 1414. They comprised books of canon law, theology and a huge Bible of the fourteenth or late thirteenth century, into which the list of his donations was entered (eight of the eleven books were still in the library in 1944).

Most of what we know about the 551 medieval volumes in the Municipal Library in 1890 comes from the catalogue published in that year, but there are other sources of information too. Between 1890 and 1944 many scholars studied this material, from one point of view or another. In 1905 the priest and scholar Marcel Langlois (1871–1941) published an article on the scribes of Chartres, surveying all references in the manuscripts to those who had written them. In 1929, there was a book by Yves Delaporte on the illuminated manuscripts in the collection, with twenty-four black-and-white plates. Obviously, the more photographs that were taken of the manuscripts and the more microfilms made before the war, the better the chance to continue study after their physical destruction, since such things as script and style of illustration could still be analysed. One scholar who made a major contribution in this respect was Loren C. MacKinney (1891–1963), of the University of North Carolina at Chapel Hill. He was especially interested in medieval medical manuscripts and made regular trips to Europe to secure photographs and microfilms of them. In 1937, he published *Early Medieval Medicine with Special Reference to France and Chartres*.

His slides, photographs and research notes are preserved at the University of North Carolina, the slides being digitized in 2007. MacKinney left images from twenty-nine of the Chartres books. One example is MS 313, a fourteenth-century manuscript containing Gerard of Cremona's translation of Avicenna's *Canon*. Avicenna was the name by which the Latin West knew Abū ʿAlī al-Ḥusain ibn ʿAbdullāh ibn Sīnā, one of the most important philosophers and medical writers of medieval Islam, who lived in Iran and central Asia and died in 1037. His *Canon* is a medical encyclopaedia, summarizing much of the teaching of the ancient Greeks, and it is systematic and ambitious in its coverage. From the eleventh century, western scholars, realizing the greater sophistication and learning of the Islamic world, undertook a large-scale, determined campaign of translation from the Arabic into Latin. Gerard of Cremona (d. 1187) was one of the most prolific of these translators, who made his way to Spain, where Arabic, Latin and other languages existed side-by-side, and amongst many other translations, produced a Latin version of the *Canon*, which became a standard text of medical education in the Christian West. This is the text found in MS 313 at Chartres. At the end of the manuscript there is a short text, *Explanation of Some Arabic Terms*, which MacKinney photographed, and which can stand as a small symbol of the way Arabic learning flooded into the Christian West between the eleventh and the thirteenth centuries, a flood that carried with it a great deal of ancient Greek learning. This manuscript of Avicenna's *Canon* was one of two medical books in the Chartres library that had been owned by a certain Laurence of Thumesnil (identified by MacKinney as a member of the cathedral chapter) and that were donated to the cathedral library by his executors, the other being MS 286, which contained a variety of texts translated from Greek and Arabic. One assumes that Laurence was a doctor, that Thumesnil was his place of origin (it is nowadays a suburb of Lille) and that he lived some time after the first half of the fourteenth century, when MS 286 was written. Avicenna's *Canon*, written in Arabic in central Asia and Iran in the first quarter of the eleventh century, had made its way to Spain, where an Italian scholar had translated it into Latin, catapulting it into the heart of Western medical education, so that a copy of it could be studied in northern France in the fourteenth century before coming into the Chartres cathedral library.

MacKinney, born in 1891, belonged to a generation of American medievalists who were busily engaged in expanding and professionalizing their subject. The Medieval Academy of America was founded in 1925. An original member of the Academy and its second president was Charles Homer

Haskins, professor at Harvard and a formative figure in medieval studies in America, who, in 1927, published *The Renaissance of the Twelfth Century*, a book destined to question old stereotypes of the period and to create a new model that is still being debated. Haskins rejected the idea of a medieval period that was a time of 'ignorance, stagnation, and gloom', to be contrasted with 'the light and progress and freedom of the Italian Renaissance'. 'The Middle Ages', he wrote, 'exhibit life and color and change, much eager search after knowledge and beauty, much creative accomplishment in art, in literature, in institutions.' Figures such as Thierry of Chartres and Gerard of Cremona recur in the pages of Haskins' book as examples of that intellectual and cultural vigour. In some ways the ground had been prepared for Haskins by an earlier publication from an American scholar, *Mont-Saint-Michel and Chartres* by Henry Adams, which appeared in 1904, and takes the form of a journey through the eleventh, twelfth and thirteenth centuries in order to gain 'a sense of what those centuries had to say, and a sympathy with their ways of saying it'. The central section of the book is dedicated to Chartres cathedral and the cult of the Virgin. American scholars of the interwar period whose energy and funding took them across the Atlantic to study in French libraries and archives (and elsewhere in Europe) came with a mental background provided by such romantic and Francophile images. No one could have imagined American bombs falling on Chartres.

After the bombing of 1944, the surviving fragments of the manuscripts from Chartres were gathered up and sent to the National Library in Paris. The twenty-first century saw a renewed and dramatic commitment to 'Rediscovering the Manuscripts from Chartres', the title of a project of the prestigious Institute for Research and History of Texts (*Institut de recherche et d'histoire des textes*), which began in 2005. The Institute describes its programme as having several components: relaxation of the parchment leaves that had been fused or charred, digitization, identification of the texts, online presentation of the digitized images and a descriptive catalogue. The project has made major progress, with thousands of manuscript fragments now available online. Almost everything that survived the bombing of 1944 can be seen by anyone, enlarged and compared. There is also a full online bibliography, giving references to all discussions of the individual manuscripts and information on where any photographs or microfilms can be found. As much has been done as can be done to mitigate the disaster of 1944.

Conclusion

THE PAST IS NOT PRESENTED TO US ON A PLATE; IT is created. We make deductions from things that exist now, deciding to regard them as traces or indications of what happened in bygone days. These are our 'sources', and the first thing that anyone studying the past has to do is make an inventory of the relevant sources. If you study silent film, you make a list of surviving films and lost films. If the subject involves archaeology, for example, Viking swords, you need a list of sites, finds, excavations. But it is rarely the case that a study can be based on a complete body of relevant sources. The film scholar must immediately face the question not only of how we know those lost films existed, but how different the picture would be if they had survived, and the archaeologist must keep in mind, that, necessarily, you can never say that your list of Viking swords is complete. Both must be aware that their sources are partial. And there are reasons for this. Archaeologists, for example, know that their potential source material is vast, but depends on expensive methods to explore. Full excavation is slow and costly, and funding relies on the favour of states, foundations and sometimes rich individuals or companies. Even when the involvement of teams of archaeologists was actually mandated during the construction of a new high-speed railway line in England

(HS2), the archaeological results, although impressive and exciting, represent only a fraction of what there is to be discovered. And there is no reason to believe that what has been discovered is representative of what there is to be discovered (archaeology was long skewed to the archaeology of the dead, since graveyards are more likely to be open and available to excavation than built-up areas of habitation).

Nevertheless, archaeology gradually creates a new past, by investigating sites and objects previously unknown to us and by applying new techniques, such as DNA analysis. Our list of sources may be partial, but it can be extended. Does the same apply to written sources? There are of course no 'new' written sources about the past in the sense of 'newly produced' – newly produced written sources, like the Hitler Diaries, are called 'forgeries' – but there will be sources that have not been explored or analysed before. There are texts written in unknown languages, that begin to yield up their information if the language is deciphered. The demonstration by Ventris and Chadwick in the early 1950s that the mysterious script known as Linear B from Crete was an early form of Greek meant there were now useable written sources for the civilization of Minoan Crete and Mycenaean Greece in the period 1400–1200 BC. There are also works which are known to have existed at one time but were thought to have been lost – and are then found: a copy of the score for Haydn's Cello Concerto No. 1 in C major, which was presumed to have disappeared forever, turned up in the Prague National Museum in 1961, 200 years after it was composed. There are works that were previously unknown (to us) but that emerge from excavations, notably papyrus texts from the deserts of

Egypt and the Levant, but also writing on wooden tablets from the Roman fort of Vindolanda in northern England or the birchbark letters from Novgorod. There are texts that existed somewhere but were uncatalogued and unstudied, and hence 'unknown' to the world of scholarship. In the 1890s, the contents of the Cairo genizah were acquired by Western scholars and libraries, releasing hundreds of thousands of medieval texts for scholarly investigation, a process that is continuing to this day. Newly read and analysed material is likely to produce a new picture of the past.

As discussed in Chapter 3, we know that a large proportion of the manuscripts produced in medieval Europe no longer exist, and it is an important task when undertaking historical research to decide what proportion. A lack of documents does not always mean the same thing, since it may be explained by the scale of production or by the scale of destruction. To take an extreme example, we know that the relative paucity of documents from the Byzantine empire is the result of massive losses, while the documentary silence of Scandinavia in the early Middle Ages points to a world of limited literacy. The volume and nature of the written record determine the history that can be written. All the surviving written sources for Anglo-Saxon England could be put on one large sturdy table; the sources for thirteenth-century England could not be read by a scholar in a lifetime. For a thirteenth-century king, such as Edward I, we know where he was virtually every day, but for the kings of the Anglo-Saxon kingdoms, especially in the earlier centuries, it is often not possible to be sure of the dates of their accession or death. When personal letters and diaries began to be composed, in the very late Middle Ages and early modern period, a whole new kind of history can be written. Letters do survive in substantial numbers from earlier centuries of the Middle Ages, but they are literary products, public declarations, not personal or private communications.

We know, by definition, that a finite amount of written material was produced in the Middle Ages. As discussed in Chapter 3, some people have tried to estimate what that amount was, suggesting an order of magnitude around 10 million manuscripts. More important than that figure, however, which is extremely difficult to arrive at, are some well-established trends: a relative quickening of the pace in the ninth century (the Carolingian period) that was crucial for the transmission of earlier Latin literature; a steep increase in production between 1100 and 1500; and an overall level that was well below what was possible after the revolutions of printing and, eventually, mass literacy. That finite amount of written material, whatever it was, began to decrease even as it was being produced. Although parchment is tough, it is not indestructible and was subject to forces that did destroy it: it could be eaten by animals; it could be washed away in floods; most of all, it might be burned in accidental fires, since medieval circumstances created extreme flammability. Houses were made mainly of wood and thatch, while naked flames were everywhere, as all heat came from burning wood and all light from naked flames in candles or lamps. Hence recurrent fires are just taken for granted in the period, some very serious.

Another threat to the manuscript hoard was re-use. Parchment is ideal for wrapping wet things, such as fish, or greasy things, such as butter, and it was cut up and used in this way, while after the spread of firearms parchment was valued for making cartridges. In Protestant countries, bookbinders often used bits of parchment from medieval liturgical manuscripts as covers or strengthening when they bound loose papers or made printed books. This destroyed the integrity of the medieval book, of course, but paradoxically ensured that parts of the text would survive, since such re-used material can often still be read, especially if the bound papers or printed books are at some point rebound and the medieval fragments separated. Hardly any liturgical books survive from medieval Norway, but, reused in bindings, there are 6,500 fragments, which originate in about a thousand different service books, going back as far as the eleventh century. A project at the University of Bergen dedicated to the study of such material ran from 2012 to 2017, part of a scholarly enterprise that has revolutionized the liturgical evidence available for medieval Norway. Scholars investigated the musical notation, the international connections, the scribes and many other aspects of this material, and the work is ongoing. A similar project has been undertaken at Canterbury.

In addition to accidental or incidental threats to the transmission of medieval writing, there were also purposeful acts of destruction. As we have seen in Chapter 5, there might be arson when popular risings occurred. But arson is limited if it is only a conflagration started by flint and torch. Explosive power is far more destructive. This was introduced to western European warfare in the fourteenth century, with the arrival of gunpowder, the 'powder of hell' in Milton's words, and was first used to propel solid shot, but it could also blow things up – as was planned in the Gunpowder Plot of 1605, when the English Parliament had a narrow escape. Francis Bacon had noted gunpowder, along with printing and the mariner's compass, as markers of modernity (see Chapter 1), and Renaissance humanists sometimes contrasted printing and gunpowder as 'invented through divine inspiration and through diabolic suggestion'. Greater destructive power developed with the invention of projectiles that exploded over their target or detonated on impact, then with the vast increase of explosive power and finally with aerial warfare, the bomber and the missile. It was now possible for huge conflagrations of medieval manuscripts to take place in a few hours – the chief subject of this book. Scholars of 1900 had the possibility of looking at medieval manuscripts that scholars of today will never see.

At the same time as destruction through attrition, arson and explosion, there has been a countervailing force: work on preserving manuscripts of the past, on analysing them and reproducing them through various techniques. One should remember with gratitude the work of conservation and recording carried on by many individuals over the years. There are heroes of transcription, editing and cataloguing: Sir James Ware collecting and transcribing medieval manuscripts in seventeenth-century Dublin, Gaetano Carcani in eighteenth-century Naples arranging the printing of the documents of the medieval emperor Frederick II, Count Bastard learning lithography in the 1830s in order to publish images of medieval illustrations, Henri Omont and his colleagues preparing their meticulous catalogue of the contents of the Municipal Library in Chartres in the 1880s, Herbert Wood inventorying the contents of the Public Record of Ireland as guerrilla warfare raged around him. Reproductive technologies like printing, photography, microfilm and, more recently, digitization have developed and can ensure that future destructions – which must happen – will never be total. There are also the archivists and other scholars involved in making good, as far as possible, the damage done. The catastrophes in Dublin, Naples and Chartres have all been followed by decades of meticulous reconstructive work. The development of science and technology has made destruction much more powerful but also given amazing new tools for such reconstruction, making charred remains from a century ago legible again. *The Garden of Delights* and the Ebstorf Map, although neither now exists, have been recreated as far as they can be, and both continue to throw light on the medieval world.

Manuscripts were kept for various reasons. One may, once again, distinguish archives and libraries. Archives were originally practical and useful. Title deeds, for instance, were preserved in case there was a challenge to the possessor's right. The annual audit of the income of the king of England, written down in the so-called Pipe Rolls, enabled the royal administration to keep an eye on what was owed and to check on local officials. Records of outgoing documents allowed the government that issued those documents to verify any claims or disputes involving them. But it is not clear why documents were kept for years or centuries after that practical purpose no longer existed. It might have been partly from inertia, since it is easier not to throw things away than it is to throw them away, or there may have been uncertainty about how long they mattered practically. Whatever the reason, at some point they became matters of purely historical interest. This was a vital moment. Were there, at that time, people who valued documents of the past as a historical record, and did those people have enough influence to ensure that time and money were expended on preserving them? The earliest surviving letter written in English, dating from the tenth century, is preserved in the archive of Canterbury cathedral. At some point in the twelfth century a monk of Canterbury annotated it – 'useless'. In his eyes it no longer had a practical purpose. But, useless or not, it has been allowed the tiny storage space it requires until the present, 1,100 years after it was written. How many similar documents were discarded or recycled?

Libraries were a different matter. Books were kept insofar as they were valuable and useful, and what is regarded as valuable and useful changes over time. By far the most important libraries of the Middle Ages were those attached to the monasteries and great churches, and naturally their collections had a focus on biblical, theological and liturgical material. In times of religious disruption, such as the Protestant Reformation and the French Revolution, monasteries became vulnerable, and destruction or dispersal of ecclesiastical books was often the result. The different ways in which church libraries were treated – the greedy mayhem of the English Reformation or the systematic planning (however imperfect) of Bavarian secularization, as discussed in Chapter 3 – made a difference to what was saved and what was lost.

The formation of national archives and national libraries is an especially important part of the story of the preservation and transmission of the past. Some of them were the creation of the revolutionary period after 1789 (a period that also, however, led to the destruction of many records of the past). The French National Archives, founded in 1790, and the State Archive of Naples, founded in 1808, are examples of revolutionary or Napoleonic foundations. Others, such as the Public Record Office, which was founded in London in 1838, were the product of the confident bureaucratic state of the nineteenth century and emerged alongside national and public museums, art galleries, concert halls, parks. Nationalism was an important force in these developments, as the example of Giuseppe Del Giudice, cited in Chapter 8, illustrates: in his opinion, study of the archives would allow the national story to be told and would further national unity. This link between nation and the study of the past was general in Europe. Nationalism, especially romantic nationalism, is historical, and hence archives and old manuscripts were valued as treasuries of the national story. Sometimes the 'national' label was only secured with a struggle. The National Library of France was first given that title in 1792, but then became the Imperial Library under Napoleon, the Royal Library under the restored Bourbons, then briefly the National Library again in 1849 during the Second Republic, before becoming the Imperial Library again under Napoleon III (1852–70), finally resuming its national title once more after Napoleon's overthrow in 1870. The British Library, which was originally part of the British Museum, founded in 1753, has never borne the title 'National', but does style itself 'British' (rather than, for example, 'English'), taking the name of the state, Great Britain, that had only been its official designation for forty-six years when the Museum was founded. The Public Record Office in London was merged into the newly formed 'The National Archives' in 2003, although which 'nation' the name refers to is not specified.

Nationalism not only created great central archives and libraries but was also a force that generated war and chaos, as nation states clashed, minority peoples fought for independence or conflicts took place in regions of mixed nationalities. The creation of the German empire in 1871 had as collateral damage the destruction of *The Garden of Delights*, one of the most remarkable illuminated manuscripts produced in medieval Germany. The struggle for Irish national independence in the early twentieth century involved, as a by-product, the incineration of the bulk of Ireland's medieval records. The centralization of archives and libraries in the form of national archives and national libraries promised greater access to the records of the past, but it also created new vulnerabilities. These institutions tended to be situated in important cities, often capital cities, exactly the kind of place that would be targeted by invading armies and bombed in aerial warfare. If *The Garden of Delights* had stayed in some remote religious house rather than being moved to the town library of Strasbourg (the capital of the département), or if the Ebstorf Map had stayed in Ebstorf, where it had been for more than 500 years, rather than coming to the State Archive in Hanover, they would probably have survived the wars that destroyed them. The state can preserve, but it can also destroy. What we can know of the past depends on what has been handed down, and that is not a constant. We make the past, but we can also lose it.

Figures

189

Abbreviations

BL	British Library, London
BnF	Bibliothèque nationale de France, Paris
fol.	folio
HD	*The Hortus deliciarum of Herrad of Hohenbourg*, ed. Rosalie Green et al. (2 vols., London, 1979)
MGH	Monumenta Germaniae historica
MS	manuscript
ODNB	*Oxford Dictionary of National Biography* (60 vols., 2004)
OMT	Oxford Medieval Texts
RS	'Rolls Series', Rerum Britannicarum Medii Aevi Scriptores

Notes

Notes to Chapter 1: Our Knowledge of the Past

* p. 1: Document of 1398: BnF, MS Clairambault 830, fol. 1 – https:// gallica.bnf.fr/ark:/12148/btv1b54100565b/f17.item.r=Clairambault%20 830; the name 'de Courguilleroy' derives from Corquilleroy near Montargis.
* p. 1: On the history of the Clairambault collection and the events of 1792, see Philippe Lauer, *Catalogue des manuscrits de la collection Clairambault* (3 vols., Paris, 1923–32), vol. III, pp. v–xxi.
* p. 4: Gubbio tablets: Augusto Ancillotti and Romolo Cerri, *The Tables of Iguvium* (Eng. tr., Perugia, 1997).
* p. 5: Oxyrhynchus: see Oxyrhynchus Online.
* p. 5: On parchment, see Peter Rück (ed.), *Pergament: Geschichte, Struktur, Restaurierung, Herstellung* (Sigmaringen, 1991).
* p. 6: 'animal papyrus': 'in papiro ferarum', St Gallen, Stiftsbibliothek, Cod. Sang. 751, p. 184, a tenth-century collection of medical texts.
* p. 6: 'English Exchequer records were ordered to be kept on sheepskin': Richard fitz Neal, *Dialogus de Scaccario: The Course of the Exchequer*, ed. Charles Johnson (rev. ed., OMT, 1983), p. 31.
* p. 6: '645 legal deeds from the sixteenth to twentieth centuries': S. P. Doherty, S. Henderson, S. Fiddyment et al., 'Scratching the Surface: The Use of Sheepskin Parchment to Deter Textual Erasure in Early Modern Legal Deeds', *Heritage Science*, 9: 29 (2021). https://doi.org/10.1186/s40494-021-00503-6
* p. 7: Bull of Pope John VIII from 876: Joseph von Karabacek, *Das arabische Papier* (Vienna, 1887), pp. 18–20; the document is BnF latin 8840.

* p. 7: On the late use of papyrus, see Naphtali Lewis, *Papyrus in Classical Antiquity* (Oxford, 1974), pp. 92–4.

* p. 7: Colin H. Roberts and T. C. Skeat, *The Birth of the Codex* (London, 1983).

* p. 7: Parchment codex fragment found at Oxyrhynchus: this is the *Fragmentum de bellis Macedonicis*, now in the British Library, as Papyrus 745 (despite not being papyrus); there is an illustration in Michelle Brown, *A Guide to Western Historical Scripts from Antiquity to 1600* (London, 1990), no. 4, pp. 22–3.

* p. 8: Theories of the relationship between Christianity and the codex: Stuart G. Hall, 'In the Beginning Was the Book', in *The Church and the Book*, ed. R. N. Swanson, Studies in Church History 38 (Cambridge, 2004), pp. 1–10.

* p. 9: The speed of scribes: Johann Peter Gumbert, 'The Speed of Scribes', in *Scribi e colofoni: Le sottoscrizioni di copisti dalle origini all'avvento della stampa: Atti del seminario di Erice – X Colloquio del Comité international de paléographie latine (23–28 ottobre 1993)*, ed. Emma Condello and Giuseppe de Gregorio (Spoleto, 1995), pp. 57–69.

* p. 9: 'One elderly scribe': Antoine Brix, 'Note sur la vitesse d'écriture d'un vieux scribe breton du XVe siècle: Copier les *Grandes Chroniques de France* dans le manuscrit Paris, BnF, fr. 4984', *Annales de Bretagne et des pays de l'Ouest*, 126: 3 (2019), pp. 7–19.

* p. 9: '200 lines a day': Michael Gullick, 'How Fast Did Scribes Write? Evidence from Romanesque Manuscripts', in *Making the Medieval Book: Techniques of Production*, ed. Linda L. Brownrigg (Los Altos Hills and London, 1995), pp. 39–58, concluding that 200 lines a day would be a good day's work for a Romanesque scribe, a figure repeated in Nigel Morgan and Rodney M. Thomson (eds.), *The Cambridge History of the Book in Britain II: 1100–1400* (Cambridge, 2008), p. 83.

* p. 9: Christine de Pisan: Gilbert Ouy, 'Une Énigme codicologique: Les signatures des cahiers dans les manuscrits autographes et originaux de Christine de Pisan', in *Calames et Cahiers: Mélanges de codicologie et de paléographie offerts à Léon Gilissen*, ed. Jacques Lemaire and Émile Van Balberghe

(Brussels, 1985), pp. 119–31, at p. 126: 'Ci commence .j. quayer escript en jour trestout.' The manuscript is Brussels, Bibl. Royale MS 9508, a copy of Christine's *La Mutacion de Fortune*.

* p. 9: St Martin in Tournai: 'Scriptorum quippe copiam a Domino sibi datam exultabat, ita ut, si claustrum ingredereris, videres plerumque 12 monachos iuvenes in cathedris sedentes et super tabulas diligenter et artificiose compositas cum silentio scribentes. Unde omnes libros Ieronimi in explanatione prophetarum omnesque libros beati Gregorii et quoscumque invenire potuit beati Augustini, Ambrosii, Hysidori, Bede, necnon etiam domni Anselmi, tunc temporis abbatis Beccensis, postea vero Canthuariensis archiepiscopi, tam diligenter fecit describi, ut vix in aliqua vicinarum ecclesiarum similis inveniretur bibliotheca, omnesque pro corrigendis libris suis de nostra ecclesia peterent exemplaria': Hermann of Tournai, *Liber de restauratione ecclesie Sancti Martini Tornacensis*, 79 (80), ed. R. B. C. Huygens, Corpus Christianorum, Continuatio Mediaevalis, 236 (Turnhout, 2010), pp. 133–4.

* p. 11: On the *pecia* system and the Parisian book trade, see Richard H. Rouse and Mary A. Rouse, *Manuscripts and Their Makers: Commercial Book Producers in Medieval Paris, 1200–1500* (2 vols., London, 2000).

* p. 12: Writing on paper 30 per cent faster: Johann Peter Gumbert, 'The Speed of Scribes', in *Scribi e colofoni: Le sottoscrizioni di copisti dalle origini all'avvento della stampa: Atti del seminario di Erice – X Colloquio del Comité international de paléographie latine (23–28 ottobre 1993)*, ed. Emma Condello and Giuseppe De Gregorio (Spoleto, 1995), pp. 57–69, at p. 62.

* p. 12: On the dissemination of paper, see Jonathan Bloom, *Paper before Print: The History and Impact of Paper in the Islamic World* (New Haven, 2001).

* p. 13: Byzantine paper: Franz Dölger and Johannes Karayannopulos, *Byzantinische Urkundenlehre: 1. Abschnitt: Die Kaiserurkunden* (Munich, 1968), p. 27; Christian Gastgeber, 'Die Überlieferung der griechischen Literatur im Mittelalter', in *Einführung in die Überlieferungsgeschichte und in die Textkritik*

der antiken Literatur, II: *Mittelalter und Neuzeit*, ed. Egert Pöhlmann (Darmstadt, 2003), pp. 1–46, at pp. 7, 14.

* p. 13: John Tate: Richard L. Hills, 'Tate, John (c. 1448–1507/8), Merchant and Paper Maker', *ODNB*, 53, pp. 809–10.

* p. 13: 'if it is paper, I will give eight florins': 'de biblia emunda hoc est desiderium meum: si papirea est, octo florenos dabo, si est in pergameno, duplum': Aeneas Silvius Piccolomini (later Pope Pius II), *Epistularium – Epistulae priuatae quas ante sacerdotium composuit (1431–1445)*; epist. 178 (Eneas Silvius to Johann Tuschek in Prague; Vienna, 23 August 1445), p. 526 = *Der Briefwechsel des Eneas Silvius Piccolomini, ed. Rudolf Wolkan, 1. Abt.: Briefe aus der Laienzeit (1431–1445)*, *I. Band: Privatbriefe*, Fontes rerum Austriacarum, II, 61 (Vienna, 1909), pp. 1–595, at p. 526.

* p. 13: 'fifteenth-century paper survives today': Paul Needham, 'Book Production on Paper and Vellum in the Fourteenth and Fifteenth Centuries', in *Papier im mittelalterlichen Europa: Herstellung und Gebrauch*, ed. Carla Meyer, Sandra Schultz and Bernd Schneidmüller (Berlin, Munich and Boston, 2015), pp. 247–74, at p. 263.

* p. 14: '1,500 double-sided printed sheets': Andrew Pettegree, *The Book in the Renaissance* (New Haven and London, 2010), p. 71.

* p. 14: 'For these three things', he wrote, 'have indeed changed the face and condition of the world': Francis Bacon, *Novum Organum* (1620), bk. 1, Aphorism 129: 'Artis nimirum Imprimendi, Pulveris Tormentarii, et Acus Nauticae. Haec enim tria rerum faciem et statum in orbe terrarum mutaverunt: primum, in re literaria; secundum, in re bellica; tertium, in navigationibus: unde innumerae rerum mutationes sequutae sunt; ut non imperium aliquod, non secta, non stella, majorem efficaciam et quasi influxum super res humanas exercuisse videatur, quam ista mechanica exercuerunt.'

* p. 14: Bacon on the superiority of Europe: 'Rursus (si placet) reputet quispiam, quantum intersit inter hominum vitam in excultissima quapiam Europae provincia, et in regione aliqua Novae Indiae maxime fera et barbara: ea tantum differre existimabit, ut merito hominem homini Deum esse, non solum propter auxilium et beneficium, sed etiam per status

comparationem, recte dici possit. Atque hoc non solum, non coelum, non corpora, sed artes praestant. Rursus, vim et virtutem et consequentias rerum inventarum notare juvat: quae non in aliis manifestius occurrunt, quam in illis tribus quae antiquis incognitae, et quarum primordia, licet recentia, obscura et ingloria sunt.'

* p. 14: 'Between 1450 and 1600, 345,000 separate titles': Andrew Pettegree, *The Book in the Renaissance* (New Haven and London, 2010), pp. xv–xvi, 354, 357.

* p. 15: 'Who does not know how great is the difference between a manuscript and a printed work?': Johannes Trithemius, *De laude scriptorum* (Mainz, 1494), c. 7 [ed. Klaus Arnold, 1974]: 'Quis nesciat quanta sit inter scripturam et impressuram distantia? Scriptura enim si membranis imponitur ad mille annos poterit perdurare; impressura autem cum res papirea sit, quamdiu subsistet? Si in volumine papireo ad ducentas annos perdurare potuerit, magnum est.'

* p. 15: Helinand of Froidmont, *Chronica*, ed. Bertrand Tissier, *Bibliotheca Patrum Cisterciensium*, vol. VII (Bonnefont, 1669), pp. 72–205; Corneille H. Kneepkens, 'The Odyssey of the Manuscripts of Helinand's Chronicon', *Sacris Erudiri*, 52 (2013), pp. 353–84.

* p. 16: Marshall McLuhan, *The Gutenberg Galaxy* (Toronto, 1962), p. 142.

Notes to Chapter 2: Libraries and Archives

* p. 18: For some acute comments on archives and libraries, see Michael Clanchy, *From Memory to Written Record: England 1066–1307* (3rd ed., Chichester, 2013), pp. 156–73.

* p. 20: Library of Charles V: Léopold Delisle, *Recherches sur la librairie de Charles V, roi de France, 1337–1380* (2 vols., Paris, 1907, repr. Amsterdam, 1967); *La Librairie de Charles V*, Bibliothèque nationale de France (Paris, 1968); Marie-Hélène Tesnière, 'La Librairie modèle,' in *Paris et Charles V: Arts et architecture*, ed. Frédéric Pleybert (Paris, 2001), pp. 225–33.

NOTES

* p. 21: 'the book collection of Mattias Corvinus': Martyn Rady, 'The Corvina Library and the Lost Royal Hungarian Archive', in *Lost Libraries: The Destruction of Great Book Collections since Antiquity*, ed. James Raven (Basingstoke and New York, 2004), pp. 91–105, at p. 92.
* p. 21: Duke Humphrey's donation: for the total number of books given by the duke, see M. B. Parkes, 'The Provision of Books', in *The History of the University of Oxford, 2: Late Medieval Oxford*, ed. J. I. Catto and R. Evans (Oxford, 1992), pp. 407–83, at 473–80; the quotation is from *Epistolae academicae Oxon.*, ed. Henry Anstey, Oxford Historical Society 35 (Oxford, 1898), vol. I, p. 177, no. 141.
* p. 21: Sorbonne: Richard H. Rouse, 'The Early Library of the Sorbonne (I)', *Scriptorium*, 21 (1967), pp. 42–71.
* p. 22: British Medieval Library Catalogues: www.thebritishacad emy.ac.uk/projects/academy-research-projects-corpus-british-medieval-library-catalogues/.
* p. 22: Augsburg: Klaus Klein, review of Sigrid Krämer, *Handschriftenerbe des deutschen Mittelalters* (2 vols., Munich, 1989; index vol., 1990), *Zeitschrift für deutsches Altertum und Literatur*, 121 (1992), pp. 216–30, at p. 216.
* p. 23: 'In 1323, the English royal treasurer': the preface to Bishop Walter Stapledon's survey of royal records, 1320–3: *The Antient Kalendars and Inventories of the Treasury of His Majesty's Exchequer*, ed. Francis Palgrave (3 vols., London, 1836), vol. I, p. 1.
* p. 24: 'in July 1318': 'una casa de volta en aquell loch on solia ésser la capeyla sua del palau de Barchinona, en la qual cassa fossen possats e conservats los registres, els privilegis e altres scrits de la sua cancelleria e dels altres fets de la sua cort': Archivo de la Corona de Aragón, Real Patrimonio, Maestre Racional, vol. 627, fols. 137v–138r (online).
* p. 24: Cava: *Codex Diplomaticus Cavensis* (12 vols. to 2015).
* p. 25: On cartularies, see Olivier Guyotjeannin, Laurent Morelle and Michel Parisse (ed.), *Les Cartulaires: Actes de la table ronde organisée par l'Ecole nationale des chartes* (Paris, 1993); Adam J. Kosto and Anders Winroth (ed.), *Charters, Cartularies and Archives: The Preservation and Transmission of Documents in*

the Medieval West (Toronto, 2002); Patrick Geary, 'Medieval Archivists as Authors: Social Memory and Archival Memory,' in *Archives, Documentation and Institutions of Social Memory* (Ann Arbor, 2006), pp. 106–13; Daniel Le Blévec (ed.), *Les Cartulaires méridionaux* (Paris, 2006); on numbers of English cartularies, *Medieval Cartularies of Great Britain and Ireland*, ed. G. R. C. Davis, revised Claire Breay, Julian Harrison and David M. Smith (London, 2010).

* p. 25: Hemming: *Hemingi Chartularium Ecclesiae Wigorniensis*, ed. Thomas Hearne (2 vols., Oxford, 1723), vol. I, p. 282.
* p. 26: Nothelm in Rome: Bede, *Historia ecclesiastica gentis Anglorum*, preface, ed. Bertram Colgrave and R. A. B. Mynors (OMT, 1969), p. 4.
* p. 27: Gregory's letters still in the archive: 'ad plenitudinem scrinii vestri recurrens, tot charticios libros epistolarum ejusdem Patris, quot annos probatur vixisse, revolvat': John the Deacon, *Life of Gregory the Great*, preface, *Patrologia latina*, LXXV, col. 62 (cf. ibid., 4.71, col. 223).
* p. 27: On the transmission of Gregory's letters, see Gregory I, *Registrum epistolarum*, ed. Paul Ewald and Ludo Hartmann, MGH, Epistolae 1–2 (2 vols., Berlin, 1887–99), vol. II, pp. vii–xxvii. On doubt about whether they were rolls or books, see Dietrich Lohrmann, *Das Register Papst Johannes' VIII (872–882): Neue Studien zur Abschrift Reg. Vat. 1, zum verlorenen Originalregister und zum Diktat der Briefe* (Tübingen, 1968), p. 186.
* p. 27: *Register of John VIII*, ed. Erich Caspar, MGH, Epistolae 7 (Karolini aevi 5) (Berlin, 1928), pp. 1–312; and Lohrmann, as in the previous note.
* p. 27: Gregory VII: Gregory VII, *Registrum*, ed. Erich Caspar, MGH, Epistolae selectae 2 (2 parts, Berlin, 1920–3).
* p. 28: Document of 1226 for Aachen: *Die Urkunden Friedrichs II.: 1222–1226*, ed. Walter Koch, MGH, Diplomata regum et imperatorum Germaniae 14, part 5.1 (Wiesbaden, 2017), no. 1190, pp. 633–7.

* p. 29: Christian Quix, *Die königliche Kapelle und das ehemalige adelige Nonnenkloster auf dem Salvators-Berge* (Aachen, 1829), pp. 80–5.

* p. 32: 542 surviving documents: *Die Urkunden Friedrichs II.: 1222–1226* (as two notes above), p. xi.

* p. 32: 'fragment from the register of his chancery for the year 1239–40': *Il registro della cancelleria di Federico II del 1239–1240*, ed. Cristina Carbonetti Vendittelli (2 vols., Rome, 2002); the examples cited are nos. 300, 335, 867. This fragment was the only surviving register of outgoing documents actually from Frederick's chancery, but a transcript of various register entries from 1230 to 1248 was made under the Angevin regime and survives in a manuscript in Marseilles (the Angevins also ruled Provence): *Acta imperii inedita seculi XIII*, ed. Eduard Winkelmann (Innsbruck, 1880), pp. 599–720 ('Registrorum Fridericianorum Excerpta Massiliensia').

* p. 33: Carcani's edition of the register: Gaetano Carcani, *Constitutiones regum regni utriusque Siciliae, mandante Friderico II imperatore* (Naples, 1786), pp. 233–420; on Carcani, see Maria Gabriella Mansi, *La Stamperia Reale di Napoli, 1748–1860* (Naples, 2002) (see index for entries) and, for some details of his time in France, Luce Courville, 'Les Bibliothécaires de la Bibliothèque Municipale de Nantes au XIXe siècle: De Carcani de Naples, à Péhant de Guérande', *Bulletin de la Société archéologique et historique de Nantes et de Loire-Atlantique*, 102 (1963), pp. 3–24, at pp. 4–7 (although Courville was unaware of the grounds for Carcani's departure from Naples).

* p. 34: 'the wonder of the world': Matthew Paris, *Chronica majora*, ed. Henry R. Luard (7 vols., RS, 1872–84), vol. V, p. 190.

* p. 35: Ernst Kantorowicz, *Kaiser Friedrich der Zweite* (Berlin, 1927); *Frederick the Second 1194–1250*, tr. E. O. Lorimer (London, 1931), quotes at pp. 678, 688–9.

* p. 35: Sthamer: Hubert Houben, 'Eduard Sthamer (1883–1938): Werdegang und Lebenswerk eines deutschen Mediävisten', in *Beiträge zur Verfassungs- und Verwaltungsgeschichte des Königreichs Sizilien im Mittelalter* (Aalen 1994), pp. ix–xviii.

* p. 37: Heupel: G. Opitz, 'Wilhelm Heupel', *Deutsches Archiv*, 8 (1951), pp. 255–6.

Notes to Chapter 3: What Has Been Lost?

* p. 38: Aeschylus' lost plays: Matthew Wright, *The Lost Plays of Greek Tragedy 2: Aeschylus, Sophocles and Euripides* (London, 2019).
* p. 39: Byzantine documents: Mark Whittow, *The Making of Orthodox Byzantium, 600–1025* (Basingstoke, 1996), pp. 1–3 (quote re 'Anglo-Saxon England', p. 3).
* p. 40: Tim O'Neill on Photius' *Bibliotheca*: https://historyforathe ists.com/2017/10/lost-books-photius-bibliotheca/
* p. 40: Catalogue from Würzburg: David Ganz, 'Book Production in the Carolingian Empire and the Spread of Caroline Minuscule', in *The New Cambridge Medieval History*, ed. Rosamond McKitterick (Cambridge, 1995), vol. II, pp. 786–808, at p. 787. For further discussion, with an illustration of the list, see Rosamond McKitterick, 'Anglo-Saxon Links with Rome and the Franks in the Light of the Würzburg Book-list', in *Manuscripts in the Anglo-Saxon Kingdoms: Cultures and Connections*, ed. Claire Breay and Joanna Story (Dublin, 2021), pp. 86–97.
* p. 40: St Augustine's: *St Augustine's Abbey, Canterbury*, ed. B. C. Barker-Benfield, Corpus of British Medieval Library Catalogues 13 (3 vols., London, 2008) vol. I, pp. lvi–lvii, 91; Neil R. Ker, 'The Migration of Manuscripts from the English Medieval Libraries', *The Library*, Fourth Series, 23: 1 (June 1942), p. 6 (repr. in his *Books, Collectors and Libraries: Studies in Medieval Heritage*, ed. A. G. Watson [London 1985], pp. 459–70), gives the number of surviving books as 165; 17 more were added in *Medieval Libraries of Great Britain: A List of Surviving Books*, ed. N. R. Ker, *Supplement to the Second Edition*, ed. Andrew G. Watson (London, 1987), pp. 12–13, and this is the figure used in Eltjo Buringh, *Medieval Manuscript Production in the Latin West: Explorations with a Global Database* (Leiden, 2011), p. 480.

* p. 40: John Bale, *The Laboryouse Journey* (London, 1549), preface, fol. B.i (spelling modernized).
* p. 41: Survival rate: Corpus of British Medieval Library Catalogues. For a general survey with an extensive bibliography, see Richard Sharpe, 'Dissolution and Dispersion in Sixteenth-Century England: Understanding the Remains', in *How the Secularization of Religious Houses Transformed the Libraries of Europe*, ed. Cristina Dondi, Dorit Raines and Richard Sharpe, Bibliologia 63 (Turnhout, 2022), pp. 39–66.
* p. 41: Joseph II: Friedrich Buchmayr, 'Secularization and Monastic Libraries in Austria', in *Lost Libraries: The Destruction of Great Book Collections since Antiquity*, ed. James Raven (Basingstoke and New York, 2004), pp. 145–62; Jeffrey Garrett, 'The Expropriation of Monastic Libraries in German-Speaking Europe, 1773–1817', in *How the Secularization of Religious Houses Transformed the Libraries of Europe*, ed. Cristina Dondi, Dorit Raines and Richard Sharpe, Bibliologia 63 (Turnhout, 2022), pp. 83–97.
* p. 42: *Bayern ohne Klöster? Die Säkularisation 1802/03 und die Folgen: Eine Ausstellung des bayerischen Hauptstaatsarchivs, München, 22. Februar bis 18. Mai 2003* (Munich, 2003), pp. 122–30, 'Die Zerstreuung der Klosterbibliotheken'; also Garrett, as in the previous note.
* p. 43: Ganz, 'Some 500 manuscripts': David Ganz, 'Book Production in the Carolingian Empire and the Spread of Caroline Minuscule', in Rosamund McKitterick (ed.), *The New Cambridge Medieval History* (Cambridge, 1995), vol. II, pp. 786–808, at p. 786.
* p. 43: David Crook, *Records of the General Eyre* (London, 1982), pp. 13–14 (data), p. 24 (quote).
* p. 45: 1257: *Close Rolls of the Reign of Henry III 1256–9* (London, 1932), p. 281.
* p. 45: Michael Clanchy, *From Memory to Written Record: England 1066–1307* (3rd ed., Chichester, 2013), p. 62.
* p. 46: 'Pioneering work': Carla Bozzolo and Ezio Ornato, *Pour une histoire du livre manuscrit au Moyen Âge: Trois essais de*

codicologie quantitative (Paris, 1980; a version with a Supplement was published in 1983).

* p. 46: Bischoff: Rosamund McKitterick, *The Carolingians and the Written Word* (Cambridge, 1989), p. 163; Wesley M. Stevens, 'Computer Databases for Early Manuscripts', in *Encyclopedia of Library and Information Science*, ed. Allen Kent, vol. LVI, Supplement 19 (Boca Raton, Fla., 1995), pp. 86–107, at p. 86.

* p. 46: Uwe Neddermeyer, *Von der Handschrift zum gedruckten Buch: Schriftlichkeit und Leseinteresse im Mittelalter und in der frühen Neuzeit: Quantitative und qualitative Aspekte* (2 vols., Wiesbaden, 1998), pp. 81, 83.

* p. 47: 'treating the manuscripts of a text as if they were fossils': John L. Cisne, 'How Science Survived: Medieval Manuscripts' "Demography" and Classic Texts' Extinction', *Science*, 307 (25 February 2005), pp. 1305–7.

* p. 47: Models from ecology: Mike Kestemont et al., 'Forgotten Books: The Application of Unseen Species Models to the Survival of Culture', *Science*, 375 (17 February 2022), pp. 765–9.

* p. 48: These figures were first published in Eltjo Buringh and Jan Luiten van Zanden, 'Charting the "Rise of the West": Manuscripts and Printed Books in Europe, a Long-Term Perspective from the Sixth through Eighteenth Centuries', *The Journal of Economic History*, 69: 2 (2009), pp. 409–45, at p. 416. The fuller analysis is in Eltjo Buringh, *Medieval Manuscript Production in the Latin West: Explorations with a Global Database* (Leiden, 2011), where these same figures are given on p. 262, table 5.6. The contrast he draws with Neddermeyer is on p. 238. Neddermeyer's figure of 2,507,500 is on p. 92 of his book. The critique of Buringh's book is by Marilena Maniaci, 'Quantificare la produzione manoscritta del passato: Ambizioni, rischi, illusioni di una "bibliometria storica globale"', IASLonline (Internationalen Archiv für Sozialgeschichte der deutschen Literatur) at: www.iaslon line.lmu.de/index.php?vorgang_id=3567.

* p. 49: Reliance on N. R. Ker, *Medieval Libraries of Great Britain* (2nd ed., London, 1964, with *Supplement*, ed. Andrew G. Watson,

1987); Sigrid Krämer, *Handschriftenerbe des deutschen Mittelalters* (2 vols., Munich, 1989; index vol., 1990).

* p. 49: Fatimid Egypt: Marina Rustow, *The Lost Archive* (Princeton, 2020), p. 16, kindly brought to my attention by Hugh Kennedy.

Notes to Chapter 4: A Narrow Escape: *Beowulf*

* p. 50: The two Carolingian manuscripts of Lucretius are Leiden, Voss. lat. 30 and 94; all other medieval manuscripts are from the fifteenth and sixteenth centuries and derive from Poggio's non-extant discovery. For detailed discussion of the Leiden manuscripts, see David Ganz, 'Lucretius in the Carolingian Age: The Leiden Manuscripts and Their Carolingian Readers', in *Medieval Manuscripts of the Latin Classics: Production and Use*, ed. Claudine A. Chavannes-Mazel and Margaret M. Smith (Los Altos Hills, CA, and London, 1996), pp. 91–102.

* p. 51: Zosimus: *Histoire Nouvelle*, ed. François Paschoud (new ed., Paris, 2000), vol. I, pp. vii–ix (Photius' comment – τὴν θρησκείαν ἀσεβὴς), pp. x–xvi (dated to 498–518 or soon thereafter), pp. lxxi–lxxiv (passages on religion), pp. lxxxviii–xcii (the manuscript, Codex Vaticanus Graecus 156).

* p. 52: On Nowell, Retha M. Warnicke, 'Nowell, Laurence (1530–c. 1570), Antiquary', *ODNB*, 41, pp. 237–9.

* p. 54: 'not only from his collection of books': Stuart Handley, 'Cotton, Sir Robert Bruce, first baronet (1571–1631), Antiquary and Politician', *ODNB*, 13, pp. 624–8, citing Thomas Smith, *Catalogue of the Manuscripts in the Cottonian Library, 1696 / Catalogus librorum manuscriptorum bibliothecae Cottonianae*, ed. C. G. C. Tite (1696), p. 59.

* p. 54: Printed catalogue of the Cotton manuscripts: Thomas Smith, *Catalogus librorum manuscriptorum bibliothecæ Cottonianæ* (Oxford, 1696), p. 83; Humfrey Wanley, *Antiquae literaturae septentrionalis liber alter* (Oxford, 1705), pp. 218–19.

* p. 55: 'much more safe from fire': cited by Simon Keynes, 'The Reconstruction of a Burnt Cottonian Manuscript: The Case of

Cotton MS Otho A. I.', *The British Library Journal*, 22: 2 (1996), pp. 113–60, at p. 113.

* p. 55: Parliamentary committee: *A Report from the Committee Appointed to View the Cottonian Library* (London, 1732), pp. 4, 15.

* p. 55: The G version of the Anglo-Saxon Chronicle was Cotton Otho B XI; Nowell's transcript is now BL, Add MS 43703, pp. 199–232; the edition printed in 1644 was in *Historiae Ecclesiasticae Gentis Anglorum Libri V*, ed. Abraham Wheloc (Cambridge, 1643–4), pp. 503–62, as *Chronologia Anglo-Saxonica*.

* p. 56: Both Asser and *The Battle of Maldon* were in Otho A XII; the text of the former is preserved in two important sixteenth-century transcripts (Cambridge, Corpus Christi College MS 100; Cotton Otho A XII*) and in the editions by Matthew Parker, *Ælfredi Regis Res Gestae* (London, 1574) and Francis Wise, *Annales Rerum Gestarum Ælfredi Magni, auctore Asserio Menevensi* (Oxford, 1722). *The Battle of Maldon* is preserved in a transcript by David Casley, previously attributed to John Elphinstone (now Oxford, Bodleian Library, MS Rawlinson B. 203, pp. 7–12), which was printed by Thomas Hearne in 1726 in *Johannis Confratris et Monachi Glastoniensis Chronica* (2 vols., Oxford, 1726), vol. II, pp. 570–7. There is more on Otho A XII in Siân Echard, 'Containing the Book: The Institutional Afterlives of Medieval Manuscripts', in *The Medieval Manuscript Book: Cultural Approaches*, ed. Michael Johnston and Michael Van Dussen (Cambridge, 2015), pp. 96–118.

* p. 56: Wanley's description: 'In hoc libro, qui Poeseos Anglo-Saxonicae egregium est exemplum, descripta videntur bella quae Beowulfus quidam Danus, ex Regio Scyldingorum stirpe Ortus, gessit contra Sueciae Regulos' (p. 219).

* p. 58: On doubts about Thorkelín's scholarship, see Magnús Fjallda, 'To Fall by Ambition – Grímur Thorkelín and His Beowulf Edition', *Neophilologus*, 92 (2008), pp. 321–32.

* p. 58: Kemble's remarks: *The Anglo-Saxon Poems of Beowulf, the Travellers Song and the Battle of Finnes-burh*, ed. John M. Kemble (London, 1833), pp. xxix–xxx.

Notes to Chapter 5: 'Away with the Learning of the Clerks!'

* p. 60: Roger Bacon, *Opus maius*, 6, ed. J. H. Bridges (3 vols., London, 1900), vol. II, p. 217 (with correction on 3, p. 143).
* p. 60: On writing and the revolt of 1381, see Steven Justice, *Writing and Rebellion: England in 1381* (Berkeley, 1994), pp. 40–7; Christoph Mauntel, 'Charters, Pitchforks, and Green Seals: Written Documents between Text and Materiality in Late Medieval Revolts', in *Communication and Materiality: Written and Unwritten Communication in Pre-Modern Societies*, ed. Susanne Enderwitz and Rebecca Sauer (Berlin and Boston, 2015), pp. 93–112.
* p. 61: *The Parliament Rolls of Medieval England, 6: Richard II 1377–1384*, ed. Geoffrey Martin and Chris Given-Wilson (Woodbridge and London, 2005), Parliament of November 1381, nos. 45, 54, pp. 230, 234–5 (at the foot of p. 234 the translation 'masters' seems correct, rather than 'ministers' as printed).
* p. 61: Margaret Sterre: 'Et vetula quaedam nomine Margareta Sterre cineres collectos in ventum sparsit, clamando, "Abcedat clericorum pericia, abcedat": *Thomæ Sprotti Chronica*, ed. Thomas Hearne (Oxford, 1719), p. 261, from Oxford, Christ Church MS 138, fol. 2v (late fifteenth century); also in BL, MS Arundel 350, fols. 15v–18 (sixteenth century).
* p. 62: Wycliffe's ashes: 'ut ejus, cujus deletur memoria, nullum possit imposterum residuum seu vestigium apparere': Letter of Martin V of 9 December 1427, Caesar Baronius, *Annales ecclesiastici*, 28 (Bar-le-Duc, 1874), p. 55, no. 14.
* p. 62: Attack on Inns of Court: *Knighton's Chronicle 1337–1396*, ed. G. H. Martin (OMT, 1995), p. 216.
* p. 62: 'According to one account': *The Anonimalle Chronicle, 1333 to 1381*, ed. V. H. Galbraith (Manchester, 1927), p. 144.
* p. 63: 'They forced the teachers in the schools of grammar': Thomas Walsingham, *Historia Anglicana*, ed. Henry Thomas Riley (2 vols., RS, 1863–4), vol. II, p. 9.
* p. 64: Christopher Dyer, 'The Social and Economic Background to the Rural Revolt of 1381', in *The English Rising of 1381*, ed.

R. H. Hilton and T. H. Aston (Cambridge, 1984), pp. 9–42, at p. 12. Interestingly, 'document destruction' was not an important part of the Jacquerie rising of 1358: Justine Firnhaber-Baker, *The Jacquerie of 1358: A French Peasants' Revolt* (Oxford, 2021), p. 79.

* p. 64: Moze in Essex: 'Curia prima post rumorem et combustionem rotulorum': *Essex and the Peasant's Revolt*, ed. W. H. Liddell and R. G. E. Wood (Chelmsford, 1981), facsimile at VIII (a); cf. the court roll of Wivenhoe cited by Dyer (as in previous note), p. 41.

* p. 64: Limoges, 579: Gregory of Tours, *Libri historiarum decem*, 5. 28, ed. Bruno Krusch and Wilhelm Levison, MGH, Scriptores rerum Merovingicarum 1/i (Hanover, 1937–51), p. 234; Parma, 1308: Samuel K. Cohn, *Lust for Liberty: The Politics of Social Revolt in Medieval Europe, 1200–1425* (Cambridge, Mass., 2008), p. 12, citing *Chronicon Parmense ab anno MXXXVIII usque ad annum MCCCXXXVIII*, ed. Giuliano Bonazzi, Rerum Italicarum Scriptores, 11/ix (Città di Castello, 1903), pp. 145–6; and *Annales Parmenses maiores a 1165–1355*, ed. Phillip Jaffé, MGH, Scriptores 18 (Hanover, 1863), p. 745.

* p. 65: Karl Hartfelder, *Zur Geschichte des Bauernkriegs in Südwestdeutschland* (Stuttgart, 1884), p. 292 (Rötteln), p. 215 (Herrenalb); Carl Jäger, *Geschichte der Stadt Heilbronn* (2 vols., Heilbronn, 1828), vol. II, p. 44 (Herrenalb).

* p. 65: Karl Schottenloher, 'Schicksale von Büchern und Bibliotheken im Bauernkrieg', *Zeitschrift für Bücherfreunde*, 12 (1909), pp. 396–408, at pp. 378 (Schwarzach), p. 399 (Langhelm), p. 401 (Bamberg); Ludwig Müller, 'Beiträge zur Geschichte des Bauernkriegs im Riess und seinen Umlanden', *Zeitschrift des historischen Vereins für Schwaben und Neuburg*, 16 (1889), p. 116 n. 2 ('twelve volumes for a penny'); Karl Hartfelder, *Zur Geschichte des Bauernkriegs in Südwestdeutschland* (Stuttgart, 1884), p. 136 (books as fuel for stoves); Johannes Letzner, *Die Walkenrieder Chronik*, 36, ed. Fritz Reinboth (Walkenreid, 2002), p. 156 (books as stepping stones).

* p. 67: 'in the written and printed word': Karl Schottenloher (as in previous note), p. 408.

* p. 67: Peasant Utopia: 'Michael Gaismars Landesordnung', in *Quellen zur Geschichte des Bauernkrieges*, ed. Günther Franz (Munich, 1963), p. 284.
* p. 67: Rising of 1701: Antonio Bulifon, 'Qurant'hore del Principe di Macchia' (the conventional name for this rising), in his manuscript *Giornali* for 1701, fols. 6–7, cited in Giuseppe Galasso, *Il Regno di Napoli: Il Mezzogiorno spagnolo e austriaco (1622–1734)*, Storia d'Italia 15. 3 (Turin, 2006), pp. 784–5.
* p. 68: The Great Fear: Georges Lefebvre, *The Great Fear of 1789: Rural Panic in Revolutionary France* (Eng. tr., Princeton, 1983; originally published 1973), pp. 43, 97, 98, 118.
* p. 69: Burning of Jewish bonds at York, 1190: William of Newburgh, *Historia rerum anglicarum*, 4. 10, ed. Richard Howlett, *Chronicles of the Reigns of Stephen, Henry II and Richard I* (4 vols., RS, 1884–9), vol. I, p. 322.

Notes to Chapter 6: Strasbourg, 24 August 1870: *The Garden of Delights*

* p. 73: '4,000 shells': Rachel Chrastil, *The Siege of Strasbourg* (Cambridge, Mass., 2014), p. 89.
* p. 73: On the history of the libraries, see Jean Rott, 'Sources et grandes lignes de l'histoire des bibliothèques publiques de Strasbourg détruites en 1870', *Cahiers alsaciens d'archéologie, d'art et d'histoire*, 15 (1971), pp. 145–80.
* p. 73: 'an irreparable catastrophe': *The Hortus deliciarum of Herrad of Hohenbourg*, ed. Rosalie Green et al. (2 vols., London, 1979), Commentary volume, p. 37. This is the standard reconstruction of the work. It is abbreviated *HD* in these notes.
* p. 73: Originally 342 folios: on fol. 1, 'Dirre bletter ist grosz und klein cccxlii', in a fourteenth-century hand (some of the leaves are only half-size).
* p. 74: Gebwiler: 'ein Hůbsch groß Lateinisch Buch genant Ortulus deliciarum', 'Geboren von Landsperg', *S. Otilien Fürstlichen herkommens, heiligen Lebens unnd wandels Histori*

(repr. Freiburg im Breisgau, 1597), p. 71. The connection with the Landsbergs had also been asserted in 1508 by Gebwiler's contemporary, Jacob Wimpheling: *HD*, Commentary volume, p. 10. It was doubted by Guillaume Adolphe Charles Schmidt, *Herrade de Landsberg* (2nd ed., Strasbourg, 1897), p. 7.

* p. 75: 'one of the most ambitious and splendid manuscripts': *HD*, Commentary volume, p. 17.

* p. 75: Publication of 1818: Christian Moritz Engelhardt, *Herrad von Landsperg, Aebtissin zu Hohenburg, oder St Odilien, im Elsass, im zwölften Jahrhundert und ihr Werk, Hortus deliciarum: ein Beytrag zur Geschichte der Wissenschaften, Literatur, Kunst, Kleidung, Waffen und Sitten des Mittelalters* (Stuttgart and Tübingen, 1818).

* p. 75: 'one of the earliest on any medieval manuscript': *HD*, Commentary volume, p. 17.

* p. 76: 'In 1864': '"C'est vous qui avez galvanisé tous ces restes glorieux du passé et, à votre voix, tout le Moyen Âge s'est relevé dans sa splendeur et sa magnificence." Ainsi s'exprime en 1864 l'éditeur Curmer dans une lettre au comte Auguste de Bastard (archives du château de Dobert, 15 septembre 1864)', cited www.inha.fr/fr/ressources/publications/publications-nume riques/dictionnaire-critique-des-historiens-de-l-art/bastard-d-es tang-auguste-de.html, a very full account of Bastard by Jocelyn Bouquillard.

* p. 77: A. Straub and G. Keller, *Hortus deliciarum: Reproduction héliographique d'une série de miniatures, calquées sur l'original de ce manuscrit du douzième siècle par Herrade de Landsberg* (Strasbourg, 1879–99).

* p. 78: 'Hail company of virgins', etc.: *HD*, fol. 1v, pp. 2–4, texts 1–3.

* p. 79: On the *Liber floridus*, see Albert Derolez, *The Making and Meaning of the Liber Floridus* (Turnhout, 2015).

* p. 79: 'The sun becomes hotter': 'Sol dum igneus sit, prae nimio motu conuersionis suae amplius incalescit. Dum sol superior sit quam luna, et tamen a nobis maior quam luna uideatur, iam si prope nos accessisset, multo maior quam luna videretur': *HD*, fol. 9, p. 15, text 34; *Summarium Heinrici*, 5. 4, ed. Reiner Hildebrandt

(Berlin, 1974), vol. I, p. 211; Isidore of Seville, *Etymologiae*, 3. 47, 48, ed. G. Gasparotto, *Étymologies, Livre III, De mathematica* (Paris, 2009), pp. 111–13 (chapters 48 and 49 in the classic edition of W. M. Lindsay [2 vols., Oxford, 1911, unpaginated]).

* p. 80: 'What do you think of knights?': *HD*, fol. 236v, p. 398, texts 807–8, 810 (the quotations in the dialogue are from Psalm 77 (78 in the Authorized Version) and Psalm 52 (53 in the Authorized Version)); 'different view of knights': *HD*, fol. 227, p. 376, text 782; 'New Knighthood': Bernard of Clairvaux, *De laude novae militiae*, in *Sancti Bernardi opera*, ed. J. Leclerq et al. (8 vols., Rome, 1957–78), vol. III, pp. 205–39.

* p. 81: Seven Liberal Arts: *HD*, fol. 32v, p. 57, plate 18.

* p. 82: The Wheel of Fortune: *HD*, fol. 215, p. 351, plate 123.

* p. 83: The Ladder, *HD*, fol. 215v, p. 352, plate 124 (also p. 513, plate 158 – the Bastard version).

* p. 83: Hell: *HD*, fol. 255, p. 438, plate 146; Bilson, cited by Keith Thomas, *The Ends of Life: Roads to Fulfilment in Early Modern England* (Oxford, 2009), p. 231.

* p. 85: 'two full-page illustrations': *HD*, fols. 322v–323, pp. 345–6, plates 153–4.

* p. 85: Life of Odilia: *Vita Odiliae abbatissae Hohenburgensis*, ed. Wilhelm Levison, MGH, Scriptores Rerum Merovingicarum, 6 (Hanover and Leipzig, 1913), pp. 24–50; Worcester: *The Chronicle of John of Worcester*, 3, ed. P. McGurk (OMT, 1998), pp. 202–6. It is not clear whether a mosaic portrait of a saint labelled 'Odilia' in Monreale cathedral in Sicily is to be identified with the first abbess of Hohenburg: Sulamith Brodbeck, *Les Saints de la cathédrale de Monreale en Sicilie: Iconographie, hagiographie et pouvoir royal à la fin du XIIe siècle* (Rome, 2010), pp. 628–31 (no. 136).

* p. 91: Captivity of Sybil: Otto of St Blasien, *Chronica*, 41, ed. Adolf Hofmeister, MGH, Scriptores rerum Germanicarum in usum scholarum separatim editi (Hanover and Leipzig, 1912), p. 66.

* p. 92: '*publica vel regia via*': *HD*, fol. 15v, p. 27, text 64.

* p. 92: *Britannia* and *Engillant*: *HD*, fol. 14v, p. 25, text 54.

* p. 93: The Strasbourg oaths: Nithard, *Historiarum libri IIII*, 3. 5, in *Quellen zur karolingischen Reichsgeschichte*, ed. Reinhold Rau,

Ausgewählte Quellen zur deutschen Geschichte des Mittelalters 5 (Darmstadt, 1955), pp. 383–461, at pp. 438–42.

Notes to Chapter 7: Dublin, 30 June 1922: The Public Record Office of Ireland

* p. 95: For a penetrating analysis of the beginning of English intervention in Ireland, see Marie-Thérèse Flanagan, *Irish Society, Anglo-Norman Settlers, Angevin Kingship: Interactions in Ireland in the Late Twelfth Century* (Oxford, 1989).

* p. 96: 'Ireland was never conquered or subordinated': 'Hibernia ... nunquam expugnata et subacta est, nunquam externae subjacuit ditioni, usque ad annum a partu Virginis millesimum centesimum septuagesimum primum, qui fuit regis Anglorum Henrici secundi octavus decimus': William of Newburgh, *Historia rerum anglicarum*, 2. 26, in *Chronicles of the Reigns of Stephen, Henry II and Richard I*, ed. Richard Howlett (4 vols., RS, 1884–9), vol. I, p. 166.

* p. 96: 'the laws of our land of Ireland and of England': 'sicut bene scitis eedem sint et esse debeant leges terre nostre Hibernie et Anglie': *Rotuli litterarum clausarum in turri Londinensi asservati* (1204–27), ed. T. D. Hardy (2 vols., London, 1833–44), vol. I, p. 497.

* p. 99: The literature on the Irish Civil War is enormous. For a clear narrative account illustrated by hundreds of contemporary photographs, see Tim Pat Coogan and George Morrison, *The Irish Civil War* (London, 1998). For a remarkable series of explanatory maps, *Atlas of the Irish Revolution*, ed. John Crowley, Donal Ó Drisceoil and Mike Murphy (New York, 2017). On the military action at the Four Courts, informed by a deep knowledge of the buildings themselves, Michael Fewer, *The Battle of the Four Courts: The First Three Days of the Irish Civil War* (London, 2019).

* p. 99: 'The inside was a jumble of lathes': Ernie O'Malley, *The Singing Flame* (2nd ed., Cork, 2012), p. 132.

* p. 100: On Macready, see Keith Jeffery, 'Macready, Sir (Cecil Frederick) Nevil, First Baronet (1862–1946), Army Officer',

ODNB, 36, pp. 13–14. For his own account of these events, Nevil Macready, *Annals of an Active Life* (2 vols., London, 1924), vol. II, pp. 652–9.

* p. 102: Ernie O'Malley: *The Singing Flame* (2nd ed., Cork, 2012), pp. 103, 136, 139.

* p. 103: Louvain University Library: Richard Ovenden, *Burning the Books* (London, 2020), p. 115.

* p. 104: 'underneath are stores of gunpowder belonging to the Office of Ordnance': *A Report from the Committee Appointed to View the Cottonian Library* (London, 1732), p. 5.

* p. 105: 'The Public Records of Ireland, like those of most countries': Herbert Wood, *A Guide to the Records Deposited in the Public Record Office of Ireland* (Dublin, 1919), p. vii; 'The centralisation of the Public Records': ibid., p. xvi.

* p. 106: Herbert Wood, 'the method of assembling the public records under one roof was the very means of making such a destruction possible': 'Public Records of Ireland before and after 1922', *Transactions of the Royal Historical Society*, 13 (1930), pp. 17–49, at p. 49.

* p. 106: Michael Kennedy and Deirdre McMahon, *Reconstructing Ireland's Past: A History of the Irish Manuscripts Commission* (Dublin, 2009).

* p. 107: 'A list of medieval and other records that had been salvaged was published in 1928': *The Fifty-Fifth Report of the Deputy Keeper of the Public Records and Keeper of the State Papers in Ireland* (Dublin, 1928), pp. 17–24, 97–8, 133–44.

* p. 107: Ware: William O'Sullivan, 'A Finding List of Sir James Ware's Manuscripts', *Proceedings of the Royal Irish Academy: Archaeology, Culture, History, Literature*, 97C, no. 2 (1997), pp. 69–99.

* p. 107: The charter of Henry II is at Add 4787, fols. 236r–v and was printed by Ware, *De Hibernia et antiquitatibus ejus* (London, 1658), pp. 237–9; another transcript had been made by George Carew in the late sixteenth century; these are collated by Nicholas Vincent, *The Letters and Charters of Henry II* (6 vols., Oxford, 2020), vol. II, pp. 229–31, no. 1008. The charter of William Marshal is at Add 4787, fols. 27–8 and is printed in *The Acts and*

Letters of the Marshal Family, ed. David Crouch, Camden Fifth Series, 47 (Cambridge, 2015), pp. 276–9, no. 162.

* p. 108: Cartularies owned by Ware: *Medieval Cartularies of Great Britain and Ireland*, ed. G. R. C. Davis, revised Claire Breay, Julian Harrison and David M. Smith (London, 2010), nos. 1376–8, 1380–1, 1383, 1387, 1394; extracts transcribed by or for Ware from nos. 1370, 1375, 1384–6, 1388, 1393 (all now 'untraced' except for 1375 and 1388).

* p. 108: On the British Record Commission, see Peter Walne, 'The Record Commissions 1800–37', in Felicity Ranger (ed.), *Prisca Munimenta: Studies in Archival and Administrative History Presented to Dr A. E. J. Hollaender* (London, 1973), pp. 9–18 (reprinted from the *Journal of the Society of Archivists*, 2: 1 (1960), pp. 8–16).

* p. 109: 'history of the Irish record commission': Margaret Griffith, 'The Irish Record Commission 1810–30', *Irish Historical Studies*, 7: 25 (1950), pp. 17–38, at p. 28. She lists the products of the Commission's work on pp. 29–35. There is an obituary of Margaret Griffith in *Analecta Hibernica* 40 (2007).

* p. 110: *Facsimiles of National Manuscripts of Ireland*, ed. J. T. Gilbert (4 parts in 5 vols., Dublin, 1874–84).

* p. 110: James F. Lydon, 'Survey of the Memoranda Rolls of the Irish Exchequer, 1294–1509', *Analecta Hibernica*, 23 (1966), pp. 49–134. One of the most important sources other than the Record Commission Calendar was transcripts made by James Frederick Ferguson. It has been pointed out that Lydon overlooked another important source, William Lynch's Repertory, in nine volumes, covering 1368 to 1714: see *Archive Fever*, no. 11 (February 2020).

* p. 112: Philomena Connolly, *Irish Exchequer Payments, 1270–1446* (Dublin, 1998); *The Statute Rolls of the Irish Parliaments, Richard III–Henry VIII* (Dublin, 2002); *Medieval Record Sources* (Dublin, 2002).

* p. 112: Paul Dryburgh and Brendan Smith, *Handbook and Select Calendar of Sources for Medieval Ireland in the National Archives of the United Kingdom*, ed. Paul Dryburgh and Brendan Smith (Dublin and London, 2005).

* p. 112: Peter Crooks, 'Reconstructing the Past: The Case of the Medieval Irish Chancery Rolls', in *Lawyers, the Law and History*, ed. Felix M. Larkin and N. M. Dawson (Dublin, 2013), pp. 281–309.
* p. 113: 'Beyond 2022': see www.virtualtreasury.ie/
* p. 114: The Yellow Book of Lecan is Dublin, Trinity College MS 1318 (H. 2. 16).
* p. 114: Katharine Simms: see the Bardic Poetry Database: https://bardic.celt.dias.ie/
* p. 115: The Llanthony survey of Irish lands in 1408 is the National Archives, C/115/80: 'Porter family, Scudamore and Fitzroy-Scudamore family, Frances, duchess of Norfolk (d. 1820), Master's Exhibit.'
* p. 115: Grant to Arthur Porter: *Letters and Papers, Foreign and Domestic, of the Reign of Henry VIII*, ed. James Gairdner and R. H. Brodie (London, 1898), vol. XVI, pp. 382–4.
* p. 116: On the Scudamores, Ian Atherton, 'Scudamore Family', *ODNB*, 49, pp. 573–6.
* p. 116: For the divorce of Frances Scudamore and the duke of Beaufort, Lawrence Stone, *Broken Lives: Separation and Divorce in England, 1660–1857* (Oxford, 1993), pp. 117–38.

Notes to Chapter 8: Naples, 30 September 1943: The State Archive

* p. 119: 'laws and statutes for the administration of the kingdom': *Codice diplomatico del regno di Carlo I. e II. d'Angiò*, ed. Giuseppe del Giudice (3 vols., Naples, 1863–1902), vol. III, p. xix.
* p. 120: 'What a fine ceremony, Delmas': Stendhal, *Lucien Leuwen*, cap. 3, Penguin ed., p. 49.
* p. 121: 'General Archive of the Kingdom': known as Archivio generale del Regno 1808–18, Grande archivio del Regno 1818–74 and Archivio di Stato di Napoli from 1874.
* p. 121: 'the use of all the archives is public': *Bullettino delle leggi del Regno di Napoli*, 2 (1808), pp. xiv, 770–5, at p. 774.

* p. 121: monastic 'parchments': *Codice diplomatico del regno di Carlo I. e II. d'Angiò*, ed. Giuseppe del Giudice (3 vols., Naples, 1863–1902), vol. I, pp. ii–iii.
* p. 121: 'Hard and arduous work': ibid., p. i.
* p. 122: Guelphs and the Ghibellines according to del Giudice: ibid., p. vii.
* p. 122: 'In 1793 a Minister of the Interior in France': Giuseppe del Giudice, *Del Grande Archivio di Napoli: Cenno storico-critico* (Naples, 1871), p. 30.
* p. 125: Count Riccardo Filangieri, 'Report on the Destruction by the Germans, September 30, 1943, of the Depository of Priceless Historical Records of the Naples State Archives', *The American Archivist* (October 1944), pp. 252–5. A full account was also printed in *The Burlington Magazine* in March 1944.
* p. 128: Evelyn M. Jamison, 'Documents from the Angevin Registers of Naples: Charles I', *Papers of the British School at Rome*, 17 (1949), pp. 87–173.
* p. 129: *I registri della cancelleria angioina ricostruiti da Riccardo Filangieri con la collaborazione degli archivisti napoletani* (50 vols., Naples, 1950–2010); the project does not appear to be ongoing.
* p. 129: Documents of 1265: *Codice diplomatico del regno di Carlo I. e II. d'Angiò*, ed. Giuseppe del Giudice (3 vols., Naples, 1863–1902), vol. I, pp. 47–8, no. XIV.
* p. 130: Galleys, etc.: Riccardo Filangieri, "Notamenti e repertori delle Cancellerie Napoletane compilati da Carlo de Lellis e da altri eruditi dei secoli XVI e XVII," *Atti dell'Accademia Pontaniana*, 58 (1928), p. 625; Riccardo Filangieri and Bianca Mazzoleni, *Gli atti perduti della cancelleria angioina: Transuntati da Carlo de Lellis*, Regesta Chartarum Italiae, 25, 31 (2 vols., Rome, 1939–42), p. 646; *I registri della cancelleria angioina ricostruiti da Riccardo Filangieri con la collaborazione degli archivisti napoletani* (50 vols., Naples, 1950–2010) vol. XXVII/1 (1979), p. 255, no. 349. The 'vaccetti' of the text are presumably 'barchetti'.
* p. 131: For reports, witness statements, etc., on the events of 28–30 September 1943, see Riccardo Filangieri, *L'Archivio di Stato di Napoli durante la seconda guerra mondiale*, ed. Stefano Palmieri

(Naples, 1996), appendix, *documenti* 2–14, pp. 19–40. Herde's analysis is in Peter Herde, 'Wolfgang Hagemann als Zeitzeuge und Zeuge im Kesselring-Prozeß (25. April 1947)', in *Italia et Germania*, ed. Hagen Keller et al. (Tübingen, 2001), pp. 51–112, at pp. 70–81. For a remarkable, if controversial, example of Herde's forensic analysis of the behaviour of a German medieval historian during the time of the Third Reich, see Benjamin Z. Kedar and Peter Herde, *A Bavarian Historian Reinvents Himself: Karl Bosl and the Third Reich* (Jerusalem 2011).
* p. 132: 'within the limits imposed by military interests': see Herde, p. 67 (in previous note).
* p. 133: 'One of the most significant archives of the West was destroyed': ibid., p. 81.

Notes to Chapter 9: Hanover, 9 October 1943: The Ebstorf Map

* p. 134: Sources for the raid: www.ndr.de/geschichte/chronologie/9-Oktober-1943-Hannover-in-Schutt-und-Asche,bombenkrieg102.html
* p. 135: *Die Ebstorfer Weltkarte: Kommentierte Neuausgabe in zwei Bänden. Band I: Atlas. Band II: Untersuchungen und Kommentar*, ed. Hartmut Kugler (2 vols., Berlin, 2007).
* p. 135: Damage to the State Archive: Manfred Hamann, 'Geschichte des Niedersächsischen Hauptstaatsarchivs in Hannover, Zweiter Teil', *Hannoversche Geschichtsblätter*, Neue Folge, 42 (1988), pp. 35–119, at pp. 78–83, 118–19.
* p. 136: For an introduction to medieval world maps, Peter Barber, 'Medieval Maps of the World', in *The Hereford World Map: Medieval World Maps and Their Context*, ed. Paul D. A. Harvey (London, 2006), pp. 1–44. For a very useful bibliography on *Mappae Mundi*, Nick Millea, 'Annotated Bibliography (1987–2018)', in Dan Terkla and Nick Millea (eds.), *A Critical Companion to English 'Mappae Mundi' of the Twelfth and Thirteenth Centuries* (Woodbridge, 2019), pp. 267–300.

* p. 136: 'God created the world': 'Diex forma le monde tout reont, autresi comme est une pelote qui est toute reonde . . . Se tel chose peüst avenir qu'il n'eüst riens seur terre, ne yaue [*read* eaue], ne autre chose qui destornast la voie quel part que l'en alast, l'en pourroit aler environ toute la terre, ou homme, ou beste, sus et jus, quel part qu'il voudroit, ausi comme une mouche iroit entour une pomme', *L'image du monde*, 1. 9, 11, ed. O. H. Prior (Lausanne, 1913), pp. 90, 93. The work is attributed to Walter or Gossouin of Metz.

* p. 138: 'First mention': Georg Heinrich Wilhelm Blumenbach, 'Beschreibung der ältesten bisher bekannten Landkarte aus dem Mittelalter im Besitz des Klosters Ebstorf', *Vaterländisches Archiv für hannoverisch-braunschweigische Geschichte* for 1834 (Lüneburg, 1835), pp. 1–21.

* p. 139: Photographs of 1891: *Die Ebstorfer Weltkarte*, ed. Ernst Sommerbrodt (text volume and 25 plates, Hanover, 1891).

* p. 140: Konrad Miller, *Mappaemundi: Die ältesten Weltkarten* (6 vols., Stuttgart, 1895–8), vol. V: *Die Ebstorfkarte*, with separate facsimile.

* p. 141: G. Magkanas, H. Bagán and J. F. Garcí, *Estudio de las miniaturas y del texto del 'Liber Feudorum Maior'* (Universitat de Barcelona, 2018); www.culturaydeporte.gob.es/archivos-aca/d am/jcr:1e686429-6b7b-4db3-a7d3-86d77c2d7e5d/lfm-informe-ub-2018.pdf

* p. 142: Gervase of Tilbury, *Otia imperialia*, ed. and tr. S. E. Banks and J. W. Binns (OMT, 2002): 'a description of the whole world', *Otia*, pref., p. 14; a *Mappa Mundi*: ibid., 1. 20, p. 116.

* p. 143: Summary of the debate on Gervase of Tilbury: *Otia*, ed. Banks and Binns (see previous note), pp. xxxiii–xxxvi (note that the identification of Gervase of Tilbury and Provost Gervase was first put forward in the seventeenth century, long before the discovery of the map); see also *Die Ebstorfer Weltkarte: Kommentierte Neuausgabe in zwei Bänden. Band I: Atlas. Band II: Untersuchungen und Kommentar*, ed. Hartmut Kugler (2 vols., Berlin, 2007), vol. II, pp. 44–7.

* p. 143: 'here rest the blessed martyrs': '*hic quiescunt beati martyres*'. The legend of the martyrs is found in various late

medieval manuscripts, for example Dresden, Sächsische Landesbibliothek: Staats- und Universitätsbibliothek, MS Dresd. H. 193 (*Chronicon episcorum Verdensium*), (old) fol. 10; Brussels, Royal Library, MS 7503–18, fols. 200–205v, and is printed in Hartmut Harthausen, *Die Normanneneinfälle im Elb- und Wesermündungsgebiet, mit besonderer Berücksichtigung der Schlacht von 880*, Quellen und Darstellungen zur Geschichte Niedersachsens 68 (Hildesheim, 1966), pp. 215–44 ('Quellenanhang'), which, as its title suggests, sees a conflation of the legend with an account of a Viking victory over the Saxons in 880. See also Bodo Gatz, 'Das Leiden der heiligen Märtyrer, die in Ebstorf ruhen', *Uelzener Beiträge*, 5 (1974), pp. 33–80; Enno Heyken, 'Die Ebstorfer Märtyrerlegende nach der dresdner Handschrift des Chronicon Episcoporum Verdensium aus der Zeit um 1331', *Niedersächsisches Jahrbuch*, 46: 7 (1974–5), pp. 1–22; Klaus Jaitner, 'Kloster Ebstorf und die Weltkarte', in *Ein Weltbild vor Columbus: Die Ebstorfer Weltkarte: Interdisziplinäres Colloquium 1988*, ed. Hartmut Kugler (Weinheim, 1991), pp. 41–53, at pp. 49–51.

* p. 144: 'earliest documentary reference': '*pro reverentia martirum beatorum Ebbekestorppe quiescentium*': *Urkundenbuch des Klosters Ebstorf*, ed. Klaus Jaitner (Hildesheim, 1985), no. 447, pp. 322–3. The indulgences were granted by 'Bernhardus ... Belonwilonensis ecclesie episcopus', a suffragan of the bishop of Verden and presumably holding a titular see 'in partibus'. A century earlier, in 1312 and 1324, there is record of a Hermann, 'Belonvilonensis ... episcopus', or 'Belonvilenis episcopus', serving as suffragan of the archbishop of Cologne and the bishop of Halberstadt: MGH, Scriptores 24 (Hanover, 1879), p. 826 (note the editorial comment: 'Quae sit, nescio'!); MGH, Constitutiones et acta publica imperatorum et regum 5 (Hanover and Leipzig, 1909–13), no. 977, p. 816.

* p. 144: Ebstorf after the Reformation: Nicolaus C. Heutger, *Evangelische Konvente in den welfischen Landen und der Grafschaft Schaumburg: Studien über ein Nachleben Klösterlicher und Stiftischer Formen seit Einführung der Reformation* (Hildesheim, 1961), pp. 123, 136, 140, 173.

* p. 144: 'medieval documents': *Urkundenbuch des Klosters Ebstorf*, ed. Klaus Jaitner (Hildesheim, 1985), p. 7.
* p. 145: Hereford Map: Scott D. Westrem, *The Hereford Map* (Turnhout, 2001).
* p. 146: Dendrochronological and stylistic analysis: Ian Tyers, 'Tree-ring Analysis of the Hereford *Mappa Mundi* Panel: ARCUS Project Report 782a' (unpublished report, 2004), with conclusion cited by Martin Bailey, 'The Discovery of the Lost *Mappamundi* Panel', in *The Hereford World Map: Medieval World Maps and Their Context*, ed. Paul D. A. Harvey (London, 2006), pp. 79–93, at p. 80; Malcolm Parkes, 'The Hereford Map: The Handwriting and Copying of the Text', ibid., pp. 107–17, at p. 115; Nigel Morgan, 'The Hereford Map: Art-historical Aspects', ibid., pp. 119–35, at p. 131.
* p. 146: 'Richard of Haldingham': 'Tuz ki cest estorie ont/ Ou oyront ou lirront ou veront,/ Prient a Jhesu en deyte/ De Richard de Haldingham o de Lafford yet pite,/Ki lat fet e compasse,/Ki joie en cel li seit done.'
* p. 147: On Sleaford as a borough: Maurice Beresford and H. P. R. Finberg, *English Medieval Boroughs: A Handlist* (Newton Abbot, 1973), p. 137.
* p. 147: On Richard de Bello: John Le Neve, *Fasti Ecclesiae Anglicanae 1066–1300, 3: Lincoln*, ed. Diana Greenway (London, 1977), pp. 20, 73; *Rotuli Ricardi Gravesend diocesis lincolniensis*, ed. F. N. Davis (Canterbury and York Society 31, 1925), p. 72; John Le Neve, *Fasti Ecclesiae Anglicanae 1300–1541, 2: Hereford*, ed. Joyce M. Horn (London, 1962), p. 38.
* p. 147: *Mappa Mundi* at Winchester: *Calendar of the Liberate Rolls: Henry III, I: 1226–40* (London, 1916), p. 405; Westminster, Robert of Melkley, Waltham: Matthew Paris, *Chronica maiora*, Cambridge, Corpus Christi College, MS 26, fol. vii^v (new foliation); Gervase of Melkley, *Ars poetica*, ed. Hans-Jürgen Gräbener (Münster, 1965); the epitaph in Matthew Paris, *Chronica majora*, ed. Henry R. Luard (7 vols., RS, 1872–84), vol. IV, p. 493. See also Dan Terkla and Nick Millea (ed.), *A Critical Companion to English 'Mappae Mundi' of the Twelfth and Thirteenth Centuries* (Woodbridge, 2019).

* p. 148: Dan Terkla, 'The Duchy of Cornwall Map Fragment (c. 1286)', in Dan Terkla and Nick Millea (ed.), *A Critical Companion to English 'Mappae Mundi' of the Twelfth and Thirteenth Centuries* (Woodbridge, 2019), pp. 197–225. He associates the map with Edmund, earl of Cornwall (d. 1300). The same handwriting has been identified on the map and on a copy of Peter Comester's *Historia scholastica* (BL Royal 3 D VI) that bears the earl's coat of arms and belonged to Ashridge, a religious house that he founded. In addition, the map fragment was later used as wrapping for manorial documents from Hemel Hempstead, a manor granted by Earl Edmund to Ashridge.

* p. 148: Monstrous races: 'Gentes que ora habent concreta modicoque foramine avenarum calamis pastus hauriunt; Mauritani Ethyopes IIII habent oculos; Sunt Hymandropedes velud semper ante cadentes' (Ebstorf); 'Gens ore concreto calamo cibatur; Marmini Ethiopes quaternos oculos habent; Himantopodes fluxis nisibus crurium repunt pocius quam incedunt et pergendi usum lapsu pocius destinant quam gressu' (Hereford): *Die ebstorfer Weltkarte: Kommentierte Neuausgabe in zwei Bänden. Band I: Atlas. Band II: Untersuchungen und Kommentar*, ed. Hartmut Kugler (2 vols., Berlin, 2007), vol. I, pp. 70, 84, 98; Scott D. Westrem, *The Hereford Map* (Turnhout, 2001), pp. 379, 385. In general on this topic, see John B. Friedman, *The Monstrous Races in Medieval Art and Thought* (Cambridge, Mass., 1981, repr. Syracuse, 2000).

* p. 150: Hymantopodes: Pomponius Mela, *De chorographia*, 3. 10. 103, ed. Carl Frick (Leipzig, 1880), p. 78; Pliny, *Naturalis historia*, 5. 46, Loeb Classical Library, tr. H. Rackham, 2 (Cambridge, Mass., 1942), p. 252; Solinus, *Collectanea rerum memorabilium*, 31. 6, ed. Theodor Mommsen (Berlin, 1895), p. 137.

* p. 151: One such eighth-century map is Biblioteca Apostolica Vaticana, Vat. Lat. 6018, fols. 63v–64.

* p. 151: Hugh of St Victor, *Descriptio mappae mundi*, ed. Patrick Gautier Dalché (Paris, 1988), p. 133: 'Sapientes uiri, tam seculari quam ecclesiastica litteratura edocti in tabula uel pelle solent orbem terrarum depingere, ut incognita scire uolentibus rerum imagines ostendant, quia res ipsas non possunt presentare.'

In Appendix I (pp. 181–92) of this edition, the editor compares the similarities of the text with both the Ebstorf and Hereford maps. For more on Hugh and maps, see Dan Terkla, 'Hugh of St Victor (1096–1141) and Anglo-French Cartography', *Imago Mundi*, 65: 2 (2013), pp. 161–79.

* p. 152: The most recent edition of Ptolemy's *Geography* is Klaudios Ptolemaios, *Handbuch der Geographie*, ed. Alfred Stückelberger et al. (2 vols., Basel, 2006).

* p. 153: 'Their bright colors, naïve legends': John K. Wright, *The Geographical Lore of the Time of the Crusades* (New York, 1925), p. 247.

* p. 153: A. L. Moir, *The World Map in Hereford Cathedral* (frequently revised and reprinted).

* p. 154: Wood from bombed churches: Scott D. Westrem, *The Hereford Map* (Turnhout, 2001), p. xix.

Notes to Chapter 10: Chartres, 26 May 1944: The Municipal Library

* p. 155: *Catalogue Général des manuscrits des Bibliothèques Publiques de France. Départements. Tome XI: Chartres*, by H. Omont, A. Molinier, C. Couderc and E. Coyecque (Paris, 1890); online at www.manuscrits-de-chartres.fr/sites/default/file s/fileviewer/documents/cgm/CGM11-Chartres-Notices.pdf.

* p. 155: Eleven manuscripts taken to the National Library in 1793: Léopold Delisle, *Le Cabinet des manuscrits de la Bibliothèque Nationale*, 2 (Paris, 1874), pp. 11–12; the fifth-century manuscript is now BnF, lat. 8907.

* p. 156: Eisenhower's directive: W. W. Rostow, *Pre-invasion Bombing Strategy* (Austin, Tx., 1981), p. 6.

* p. 156: www.americanairmuseum.com/aircraft/18398

* p. 157: Roger Joly, 'Bombardement de Chartres, 26 mai 1944', *Bulletin de la Société archéologique d'Eure-et-Loir*, 47 (1995), pp. 48–55.

* p. 158: 6,000 deaths; Free French pilot: Peter Caddick-Adams, *Sand and Steel: A New History of D-Day* (London, 2019), pp. 288–

9, citing Pierre Clostermann, *The Big Show: Experiences of a French Fighter Pilot* (London, 1951), p. 147. For the figure of 15,000 deaths, Richard Overy, *The Bombing War: Europe 1939–1945* (London, 2013), p. 574.

* p. 159: Evacuation and return of the manuscripts: Maurice Jusselin, *Petite histoire de la Bibliothèque municipale de Chartres* (Chartres, 1962), pp. 61–4.

* p. 159: Wermke: Dr Ernst Wermke (1893–1987), head of the 'Library Protection Division (*Abteilung Bibliotheksschutz*)' in France in 1940–2; Wermke's memoir: Cornelia Briel, *Beschlagnahmt, erpresst, erbeutet: NS-Raubgut, Reichstauschstelle und Preußische Staatsbibliothek zwischen 1933 und 1945* (Berlin, 2013), pp. 251 n. 504, 255–6, 342 (archival reference).

* p. 160: Fuchs' report: ibid., p. 258.

* p. 161: On Jusselin, see Jean Waquet, 'Maurice Jusselin (1882–1964)', *Bibliothèque de L'École des Chartes*, 124 (1966), pp. 643–7; his photos can be found at https://mediatheque.chartres.fr

* p. 165: For the transmission of Origen's text, see Origen, *Homélies sur les Nombres*, ed. Louis Doutreleau, 1, Sources Chrétiennes 415 (Paris, 1996), pp. 13–15; *Homélies sur le Lévitique*, ed. Marcel Borret, 1, Sources Chrétiennes 286 (Paris, 1981), pp. 52–4.

* p. 166: 'in achademia Carnotensi': Adelman of Liège, *Epistula ad Berengarium*, ed. R. B. C. Huygens, Corpus Christianorum, Continuatio Mediaevalis, 171 (Turnhout, 2000), p. 182.

* p. 166: John of Salisbury on Bernard of Chartres: *Metalogicon*, 1. 11; 1. 24; 2. 17; 3. 4; 4. 35, ed. J. B. Hall, Corpus Christianorum, Continuatio Mediaevalis, 98 (Turnhout, 1991), pp. 30, 52–4, 82–3, 116, 173–4.

* p. 167: The prologue to Thierry's *Heptateucon* was published by Edouard Jeauneau, '*Le Prologus in Eptateuchon* de Thierry de Chartres', *Mediaeval Studies*, 16 (1954), pp. 171–5; for Thierry's death and his bequest of books, see *Cartulaire de Notre-Dame de Chartres*, ed. E. de Lépinois and Lucien Merlet (3 vols., Chartres, 1862–5) vol. III, p. 206: 'Obiit magister Teodoricus, cancellarius et archidiaconus alme Marie, qui dedit huic ecclesie Bibliothecam septem liberalium artium'; there has been a long and unresolved debate about the 'School of Chartres', concerning first whether

there was any such thing and second, if there was, whether it had a distinctive outlook. See Winthrop Wetherbee, 'The School of Chartres', in *A Companion to Philosophy in the Middle Ages*, ed. Jorge J. E. Gracia and Timothy B. Noone (Oxford, 2003), pp. 36–44.

* p. 168: Figures for French paper MSS: analysis of 6,200 religious manuscripts from the North of France (i.e., biblical, patristic, theological and hagiographical texts) established that only 5 per cent of fourteenth-century manuscripts were paper, while in the fifteenth century the figure is 45 per cent: Carla Bozzolo and Ezio Ornato, *Pour une histoire du livre manuscrit au Moyen Âge: Trois essais de codicologie quantitative* (Paris, 1980), p. 57 (a version with a Supplement was published in 1983).

* p. 169: Twenty-two volumes in French: MS 212, Tancred of Bologna, *Ordinaire*; MS 271, Grandes Chroniques de France; MS 333, Somme le Roi; MS 400, Somme le Roi; MS 408, verse; MS 419 miscellany; MS 429 sermons; MS 535, Rule of Fontevrault; MSS 542–8, 550–1, nine fifteenth-century Hours; MS 620, verse fables and romances; MS 1027, miracles de Notre-Dame and Vielle chronique; MS 1152, chronicles; MS 1636, Rule of Filles-Dieu; MS 1720, fifteenth-century Hours.

* p. 170: 'eamdem ecclesiam tanquam speciale domicilium sibi elegerat in terris': Miracula beatae Marie virginis in Carnotensi ecclesia facta (BHL 5389), ed. Antoine Thomas, *Bibliothèque de l'École des Chartes*, (1881), vol. 42, pp. 505–50, at p. 509; boy at Sully, pp. 523–4; knight from Aquitaine, pp. 526–7. See, in general, Margot E. Fassler, *The Virgin of Chartres: Making History through Liturgy and the Arts* (New Haven, 2010).

* p. 171: 'Afin que ... l'entendent la gent laie': Jean le Marchant, *Miracles de Notre-Dame de Chartres. Texte établi par Pierre Kunstmann* (Ottawa, 1973) – available online at https://gallica.bn f.fr/ark:/12148/bpt6k9769582j/f106.item.texteImage. He names himself and gives the date in the final lines.

* p. 172: Amalbertus: MS 152, Augustine, *De Trinitate*, fol. 175v. Bernhard Bischoff, *Katalog der festländischen Handschriften des neunten Jahrhunderts (mit Ausnahme der wisigotischen), I, Aachen-Lambach* (Wiesbaden, 1998), p. 195, dates the

manuscript to the second third of the ninth century and gives its place of origin as Saint-Germain-des-Prés.

* p. 172: Peraldus' *Summa*: MS 204, fol. 193: 'Explicit summa de viciis. Explicit hic liber, sit scriptor crimine liber. Explicit, expliceat, ludere scriptor eat.' The same phrase occurs in MS 351, fol. 210, dated 1421.

* p. 172: MS 3, fol. 236: 'Qui legis ora pro scriptore Dodaldo clerico, si Dominum habeas protectorem'; fols. 11v–12 and 27v–28: 'Optulit hunc librum Richulfus, per manus Gisleberti, episcopi Sanctae Mariae Carnotensis ecclesiae.' On Dodaldus, see A. Wilmart, 'Dodaldus Clerc et Scribe de Saint-Martin de Tours', *Speculum*, 6 (1931), pp. 573–86. See also Bernhard Bischoff, *Katalog der festländischen Handschriften des neunten Jahrhunderts (mit Ausnahme der wisigotischen), I, Aachen-Lambach* (Wiesbaden, 1998), p. 191.

* p. 173: MS 292, fol. 149v: 'Mil e dues cenz e X et IIII s'ala Ferranz au roi conbatre' (this may have some relevance to the dating of William of Auvergne's work); fly-leaf: 'Anno Domini M°CC°L° IIII°, dominica qua cantatur: Reminiscere, computavimus de bonis ecclesie'; MS 420, fol. 309: 'Anno milleno trecenteno duodeno,/ Dum sol accubuit, terra sonans tremuit'; MS 53, 88v: 'Pioniæ radix cocta in oleo vetustissimo roseo'; MS 315: 'Ut mulier cito pariat . . . est exprobatum pro vero per me Radulphum de Verdu.' It is likely the reading is 'de Verdun'; the Bible donated by William of St-Benigne is MS 165. His other books still in the library in 1944 were MSS 219, 252, 285, 299, 309, 315, 325.

* p. 174: M. Langlois, 'Scribes de Chartres', *Revue Mabillon* (1905), pp. 158–76; Yves Delaporte, *Les Manuscrits enluminés de la bibliothèque de Chartres* (Chartres, 1929).

* p. 178: 'Rediscovering the Manuscripts from Chartres': www.man uscrits-de-chartres.fr/en

Notes to Conclusion

* p. 180: Ventris and Chadwick: John Chadwick, *The Decipherment of Linear B* (Cambridge, 1958).

NOTES

* p. 181: Vindolanda: http://vindolanda.csad.ox.ac.uk/; Novgorod: Simeon Dekker, *Old Russian Birchbark Letters* (Leiden, 2018); Cairo genizah: S. D. Goitein, *A Mediterranean Society: The Jewish Communities of the Arab world as Portrayed in the Documents of the Cairo Geniza* (6 vols., Berkeley, 1967–93).
* p. 183: 'liturgical evidence available for medieval Norway': *Latin Manuscripts of Medieval Norway: Studies in Memory of Lilli Gjerløw*, ed. Espen Karlsen (Oslo, 2013); *Nordic Latin Manuscript Fragments: The Destruction and Reconstruction of Medieval Books*, ed. Åslaug Ommundsen and Tuomas Heikkilä (London, 2017).
* p. 183: The Canterbury project: 'Rejecting and Recycling the Past in Reformation Canterbury.'
* p. 183: 'powder of hell': John Milton, *Epigrammatum Liber*, II (In Proditionem Bombardicam) ('inferni pulveris usus ope').
* p. 184: 'invented through divine inspiration and through diabolic suggestion': 'Des impressions si élégantes et si correctes sont en usage, elles qui ont été inventées de mon temps par inspiration divine, comme, à l'inverse, l'artillerie l'a été par suggestion diabolique': François Rabelais, *Pantagruel* (1532), chapter 8.
* p. 186: 'The earliest surviving letter written in English': Simon Keynes, 'The Fonthill Letter', in *Words, Texts and Manuscripts: Studies in Anglo-Saxon Culture Presented to Helmut Gneuss on the Occasion of His Sixty-Fifth Birthday*, ed. Michael Korhammer et al. (Cambridge, 1992), pp. 53–97.

Index

Medieval people are indexed under first name

bp. = bishop; kg. = king